Praise for *Awakened Leadership*

"If, as Alan Shelton asserts, awakening is akin to enlightenment, then every business person (and even those not in the corporate arena) should read this book. *Awakened Leadership* represents a bright new day in an otherwise dark world."

> —**Marshall Goldsmith,** million-selling author of *New York Times* bestsellers *MOJO* and *What Got You Here Won't Get You There*

"Many of us are perpetually engaged in the quest to better know the inner world of leadership, seeking to understand how we can rise to meet the aspirations we hold for our teams, organizations, communities, and our planet. Our challenge lies in recognizing 'what good looks like' as a seemingly endless river of leadership theory comes our way. Refreshingly, Alan opens wide a doorway and beckons us to walk with him on his personal and very touching leader's journey. It is on this journey that we experience something we did not quite expect: a new felt sense of our own authentic selves and our potential as leaders. Finally we have a leadership book—a gift, really—that gets to the heart of the matter and sparks within us a growing sense of confidence in tomorrow's possibilities."

> —**Mark Sobol,** Partner, Global Head of Sustainable Strategy & Transformation, Environmental Resources Management (ERM)

"Alan Shelton's *Awakened Leadership* inspires the revelation of our true nature so we can join hands and create what most wants to come forth—great intimacy, vulnerability, humility, and confidence—beyond what we currently know. That is real and true leadership, beyond the conceptual and into the truly experiential. The world is ripe with anticipation of this much-needed message."

> —**Ben Ames,** Senior Project Leader, Program Development, Trane

"Alan, I need to address this endorsement to you. I cannot write *about* you and your book; third person is too far from you. You are the source; you demand and deserve connection and intimacy. And this is the essence of your massive contribution to the literature of leadership and to world culture: Connect with and become intimate with the source of consciousness within your own Being. How bold, how brave, how profound! You have studied this, lived this, taught this, and now you embody this. I bow to you with great love and respect."

> —**Robert Rabbin,** self-awareness teacher, leadership advisor, author of *A Mystic in Corporate America* and *The 5 Principles of Authentic Living*

"Alan Shelton has written a book that is both compass and catalyst for transforming the nature of leadership. These concepts will likely remain out of reach for many. But for those brave enough to take the journey, Alan provides a transformational path to leadership that is essential to human, economic, and environmental sustainability."

> —**Calvin Klein,** CEO, The Nature of Business

"*Awakened Leadership* is a breath of fresh air in a world of leadership books that prescribe a magic series of steps to greater fulfillment and success. Alan's story of his journey from successful 'all-American business leader' to living an authentic life developing corporate leaders offers us keys to unlock our own unique experience of awakened living."

    —**Erik Mazziotta,** Managing Partner, IMI Conscious Leadership

"This book describes one man's search for spiritual awakening and how he manages to integrate the search with his roles as a business consultant and business leader. If you, too, are a seeker, and looking for inspiration that awakening is possible while in the midst of being a leader, this book will be a welcome companion."

    —**Barbara Braham,** PhD, MCC, Executive Coach and author of *Finding Your Purpose*

"How refreshing! A book that is an authentic personal story of a 'hard-core' business person seeking to resolve his divided self and find a way to be a more effective leader. Alan Shelton has discovered that awakening makes a much more fulfilling, expansive, inclusive, and leveraged leadership available. *Awakened Leadership* makes it easier to meet the leadership challenges before us."

    —**Sarah Cornally,** Strategic Leadership Advisor, Founder, and Managing Director, Cornally Enterprises.

"At the center of great leadership is a courageous heart. Alan Shelton has brought the heart of leadership into his book *Awakened Leadership*, and the world is truly better for it."

    —**Alicia M. Rodriguez,** President, Sophia Associates Inc.

"I was an executive for many years and have held many leadership positions. I've tried many approaches to leadership—with both dramatic success and failure. As I reflected on the stories in *Awakened Leadership*, they helped me get clear on experiences from my own past. I've always believed that storytelling is the best way to teach, and Alan Shelton is world class at both telling the story and ensuring that the golden core of insight is clear. The whole book resonated strongly with my heart . . . and soul."

    —**Hank Queen,** Consultant, Axelrod Group

"*Awakened Leadership* is a must-read for everyone, not just corporate leaders. Alan's wisdom transcends our traditional thoughts on leadership, moving us beyond our professional personas into a full, authentic existence uniting all facets of our lives."

    —**Glenn Odell,** CEO, Spectrum Information Services NW Inc.

"A bright and bold entrant into the tired annals of works on leadership, *Awakened Leadership* is a daring read for seasoned leaders willing to answer a silent call beckoning them to something greater. Enjoy this wonderfully written journey of how to 'leave the leader' and discover leadership."

—**Tim JohnPress,** Senior Consultant, Full Circle Group

"While *Awakened Leadership* is a clear indicator that Alan Shelton has lived a life of leadership viscerally and emotionally, not simply intellectually, he also manages to weave in practical strategies along the way, pointing readers toward their own awakening. This book deeply resonated."

—**Roma Gaster,** Full Circle Group, Asia Pacific

"Alan writes from the heart, sharing his own journey and inspiring leaders to bring forth their own deep well of life and leadership experience. *Awakened Leadership* is a groundbreaking book, written with courage and authenticity."

—**Gretchen M. Krampf,** MSOD, PCC, Process Experts LLC

"My time as a seeker has been that of a curious skeptic. I've read a fair amount of leadership and self-help writings, especially those that are business-focused, but I've never experienced anything like *Awakened Leadership*. I gobbled it up and found myself stretching it out as long as I could, just so I could keep Alan with me."

—**Michael Gibbons,** VP of Corporate Equipment, The Walsh Group

"Alan Shelton has written a courageous leadership book. He challenges us to experience ourselves without limits. The growing intensity and complexity of the world that leaders face today are proving our normal approaches to design and problem-solving unviable. Alan shows us how to drop the boundaries of our conditioned mind by expanding beyond our cramped, known identities, and realizing our true nature as creative energy itself. When leaders make this shift in how they see themselves, they see the world anew and find innovation everywhere."

—**Chris Thorsen,** Executive Liberation Consultant, Quantum Edge Leadership Mastery

"Just when you thought you had yourself all figured out, along comes Alan Shelton to tell you that's not the point. Read *Awakened Leadership* and learn how to go beyond personal development to an awakened state from which your leadership emerges gracefully. This book isn't just for corporate leaders, it's for everyone who leads, lives, and loves."

—**Linda Peterson,** BSN, MEd, ORSCC

"*Awakened Leadership* is a deeply personal book with a deeply personal message for all leaders who wonder how to be most effective in the biggest possible way. Alan weaves his life experience, with all its messy contradictions, into an unexpectedly neat package of realization of the oneness that unites us all. Alan reassures us that we are indeed unique players but are being lived in every moment. What a relief for the business leader to lay aside ego/doer polishing and embrace life just as it is. That's when the extraordinary happens!"
—**Bob Bunshaft,** Managing Partner, Source Consulting

"Alan Shelton shows through his own experience that it is possible—even necessary—to live and work in full alignment with a larger, non–ego-driven stance. That he has done this while serving as CEO of a successful financial services firm lands the work squarely in the leadership arena where it belongs. This is not a 'three steps to instant effectiveness' book. It is a sorely needed direction-setting guide for those of us who are busy in the world doing the best we can and are hungry for solid food."
—**Daniel Holden,** CEO, Daniel Holden & Associates

"*Awakened Leadership* is the best gift that can be given to any leader. As I read the book, I experienced Alan as my own personal coach, sitting alongside me, walking me through this unexpected, wonderful learning experience. This book points us toward a new era of leadership—and a way of leading from within."
—**Dean Hanniball,** Senior Consultant, Full Circle Group

"*Awakened Leadership* is the wild and multisensory account of a seasoned executive's journey into the land of 21st-century leadership. Shelton distills ancient wisdom into universally pragmatic approaches that ultimately invite us to become more available to our inherent greatness."
—**Shannon Schultz,** Principal, Schultz Consulting Group

"The best teachers are those that have walked a mile in our shoes. Alan's experiences shared through *Awakened Leadership* stir up our mind and heart to remind us we're not alone. All of us—leader or not—yearn for a whole life, and Alan reveals to us that it's possible."
—**Gregg Servis,** Founder, G3 Leadership Development

Awakened Leadership

Beyond Self-Mastery

Awakened Leadership

Beyond Self-Mastery

ALAN E. SHELTON

RED HATCHET PRESS / OCEANSIDE, CALIFORNIA

Book design by Joel Friedlander
www.TheBookDesigner.com

Cover design by Worthy Marketing Group
www.worthymarketinggroup.com

Editing by The Writer's Midwife, WMidwife@aol.com

Puff The Magic Dragon
Words and Music by Lenny Lipton and Peter Yarrow
Copyright © 1963; Renewed 1991 Honalee Melodies (ASCAP) and Silver Dawn Music (ASCAP)
Worldwide Rights for Honalee Melodies Administered by WB Music Corp.
International Copyright Secured   All Rights Reserved
Reprinted by Permission of Hal Leonard Corporation

ISBN: 978-0-9847125-0-2
Library of Congress Control Number: 2012901143

Red Hatchet Press, Inc.
619 South Cleveland Street
Oceanside, CA 92054-4125

e-mail: info@awakenedleadership.com

www.awakenedleadership.com

Printed in the United States of America

This book is dedicated to Odie.

He came to me an orphaned but regal mastiff.
He never needed to read or listen to any concept.
He is love.

Odie graduated this poor seeker from the living
school convened by my grandfather, by Osho
and Ramesh, and the women of spirit in my life.

There is no question of failure, neither in the short run nor in the long. It is like travelling a long and arduous road in an unknown country. Of all the innumerable steps only the last brings you to your destination. Yet you will not consider all previous steps as failures. Each brought you nearer to your goal, even when you had to turn back to by-pass an obstacle. In reality each step brings you to your goal, because to be always on the move, learning, discovering, unfolding, is your eternal destiny. Living is life's only purpose . . . The [awakened] self understands that success and failure are relative and related, that they are the very warp and weft of life. Learn from both and go beyond.

—Nisargadatta Maharaj
I Am That

Contents

To My Readers

I have chosen to include both a preface and a foreword, written by two beautiful men who are very close to me, Jerry Skillett and Bob Anderson. These extraordinary men represent the best parts of who I am. They have encouraged me to embrace and hold the two most powerful aspects of myself—plain, hard work and insightful clarity— which have become like two strands of a single rope.

Jerry and I were a one-piece band. We stood together and made up our structures as we went along. And together we learned that it is indeed possible for the human essence that yearns to express its own awakening to arise. Bob Anderson is, to my mind, a thought leader without peer. With his help, I have distilled my experience to develop the pointers that reside in the book you are about to read.

So it would be like salt with no pepper or pepper with no salt were you to read the foreword and not the preface, or vice versa, for the inspiration of these two men, and their contributions to this book, are one.

Notes to the reader often include an explanation of the author's choices regarding the use of gender-appropriate pronouns. What seems important to me, even fundamental, is to communicate how the modern concern with gender attitudes relates to the way I have shared the stories of my life. No doubt you will find in these stories an emphasis on the male side of experience. And, clearly, men and women come from different points of reference due to the nature of their DNA, conditioning, and the like.

So I humbly invite any of you ladies who would like to come along—and, of course, you gents as well—to strap yourself in for the ride. Feel free to throw rocks, spill food on yourself, and use single-syllable words. It's all part of the fun that I invite you all to share with me. I only hope that any divergence in outlook due to gender differences will be seen as an invitation to ride sidecar alongside the male experience, rather than as an attempt to separate men and women. This wish unites us all—wherever we are on the gender spectrum—in the adventures that await us in the deeper realms of experience.

Foreword

Early in my career, I met a Trappist monk for dinner one evening. His name was Reverend Vince Dwyer, and he was noteworthy for two reasons. One, he was at large, rather than living in a monastery. Health problems that required special care had forced him to leave the monastery many years earlier. The second remarkable thing about him was that he was world renowned for his work in human development, which was the reason I wanted to meet him. As we ate our meal, he told me his life story, including the events that had led to his difficult departure from the monastery and what he had done with his life since that time. Not knowing quite what to do, he studied psychology, specifically developmental psychology. In fact, he did some of the early research into the stages of adult development with Laurence Kohlberg, the founder of the field.

At the time I met him, I knew nothing about the study of adult development, so I missed the importance of what he said to me next. Vince had been a sailor before he was a monk, and he still had a sailor's mouth. With a scotch in one hand and a half-smoked cigar in the other, he said, "Bob, through that early research we discovered the same (expletive) thing that we Trappists have known for millennia—that adults can evolve, if they don't stop growing, into higher and higher stages of consciousness . . . all the way to divine union." It took me another twenty years of absorbing leadership content to understand the significance of this statement.

I spent those two decades deeply immersed in all the leadership development literature I could get my hands on, learning from some of the most influential thought leaders in the field. I discovered a random collection of really great stuff, but it lay within a field that was completely unintegrated. So I set out to integrate into a unified theory of leadership everything I was learning. It did not congeal until I revisited Vince's statement in the context of the adult development research that had been incubating off to the side of the leadership conversation. That research goes back about fifty years and includes, along with Laurence Kohlberg, people such as Carol Gilligan, Susan Cook-Greuter, Bill Torbert, Ken Wilber, Brian Hall, and Robert Kegan, to name a few.

The more I learned from these thought leaders, the more I realized that this body of work was the most inclusive framework I had come across, and that it explains a great deal about how extraordinary leadership develops. Everything I have come to know about leadership can be explained by and integrated into the framework of adult development. Now is the time for this body of work to move to center stage in our understanding about leadership.

The Unified Theory of Leadership finally coalesced around the model of the stages of adult development created by Robert Kegan, currently Harvard University's foremost researcher in the field. *Awakened Leadership* stands on the shoulders of this body of work. At the same time, it cuts new ground in the leadership conversation. Let's be clear: While Alan Shelton roots this book in the rich soil of adult development, he knows enough about the technical/theoretical complexities and nuances of the developmental stages to be dangerous. He has, however, consciously and fiercely lived through these complexities and moved into the higher levels of awareness traditionally reserved for monks (East and West). He has done so, quite remarkably, while successfully building a sizable M&A firm.

Alan is a rare combination of practical financial acumen, entrepreneurial leadership, and spiritually enlightened wisdom. So, while he may not be the person to turn to for the technicalities of adult development, he is opening a brand-new door on the leadership conversation by pointing to the experience of leadership that develops beyond self-mastery.

"Beyond self-mastery" is a radical idea. Alan leads us to what emerges at journey's end. His story reflects that no amount of self-development can take us into enlightenment—this is the paradox we meet at the end of all our efforts to improve ourselves. The self cannot transcend itself. It can only give up the quest and surrender the striver, the doer, the seeker. More striving, seeking, and doing will not suffice. You can't get there from here. In fact, engagement in more of the self-development work that has been so helpful in the past is an impediment to the awakening we seek.

Alan describes the effectiveness, capacity, power, presence, and equanimity that emerge as one surrenders the self completely. But this book is not only about the spiritual ordeal of surrender; it delivers a clear sense of the leader who naturally and effortlessly arises when there is no face to lose, nothing to gain, and when effort is desireless—in other words, when there is no self left.

For those of us who have worked our entire career to better ourselves, and for whom that effort has resulted in extraordinary development and accomplishment, perhaps it is time to realize that more of the same is likely to come up empty. Perhaps you intuit that something else is needed. And perhaps you can sense that this "something else" is an awakening beyond (or prior to) self-mastery—where the self simply rests in and as the Inherent Unity that is its source.

Einstein said that the solutions to our current (most vexing) problems cannot be found from within the consciousness that created them. Who knows what would be possible in our troubled world if leadership could emerge awakened to the presumption of a larger Inherent Unity that is the Essential Self, of which (and as which) all seeming diversity is but an exuberant expression. *Awakened Leadership* is a vital branch on the tree of this exuberance.

Bob Anderson
Founder and CEO of The Leadership Circle

Preface

For eight years, I worked side by side with Alan Shelton. It was in this setting that I came to understand the depth, compassion, competitiveness, and spirit of this truly authentic Californian. Alan is so talented that I made up a new word to describe him: "intellectuality." While not included in Webster's dictionary (so far), I define it as the ability to be engaged in the shared intellect that permeates the heart. When practiced in the leadership context, it may be the largest paradigm shift in leadership thinking ever experienced.

Alan and I spoke daily, drilling down deeply to solve the most pressing issues of the day for what turned out to be our grossly underfunded, brilliant business experiment, 24–7 digital. Minute by minute, we had to examine our path closely, deliberately, to determine whether our actions were emerging from the heart or from the head. We were seeking the "heart decisions"—the ones influenced not by textbooks, or ego, or judgment, but by whatever God was trying to accomplish through us. We were simply participants in a global, Shakespeare-scale play. We accepted whatever arose from the heart, and that's what we would say and do.

Frankly, we had no other choice. With seemingly insurmountable obstacles and virtually no resources, the only logical thing to do was to quit. However, through our being intimately present and accepting, the path kept revealing itself in all its wonder. We impacted lives—and an entire industry—and accomplished more than what was realistically possible. It didn't make any sense, yet this natural movement was all-knowing. What an awesome adventure.

Alan taught me not to think. That doesn't mean doing nothing; it means being available to quiet the endless self-talk so that the body-mind can do instinctively what it is meant to do, without getting in its own way. I suspect that artists have flashes of this; children have flashes of this; making love has flashes of this. But business? Surely not.

Wrong. Nothing could be more important and brilliant for a leader.

In the simple stories in this book, Alan has captured how life is lived *through* you. You will discover that if you choose to observe and fully participate—without judgment—in your own life, then everything unfolds naturally. In a business context, this experience is powerfully enjoyable. If every moment is perfectly orchestrated by God, why not enjoy participating in this mystery?

In sharing his experiences, Alan reveals his heart to you, entertaining and educating you at the same time. By the time you finish this book, you will recognize that Alan Shelton does not fit any leadership stereotypes. He is a choiceless thinker, a passionate man and, most important, a leader from whom there is much to learn. Intellectuality . . .

Jerry Skillett
CEO, Parkblue

Author's Preface

Many books have been written that propose to give a blueprint to humanity for how to be happy. This isn't one of them. I suppose that "happy" is a stand-in for the entire category of things that people seek—joy, peace, love, money, pleasure, fulfillment, and so on. With so many objects of pursuit, it is apparent that we are all looking for something. In fact, the common denominator of humanity seems to be a search so desperate that most people go through life in a state of perpetual bondage to this seeking. Looking everywhere except inside themselves, they cobble together a life that they imagine will be better if they succeed in changing the scenery.

In some cases, this search for satisfaction through external acquisition and achievement becomes so frustrating that an individual finally turns inward and dedicates his or her life to being a spiritual seeker. But the problem is the same for every seeker—and we are all seekers, regardless of our goals and the context of our efforts. We become trapped in a state of dissatisfaction and frustration of our own design, which I call "the seeker's hole." And we become completely convinced that unless we do all the right things, we will be stuck down there forever. We struggle like hell to get out by any means we think will work, never realizing what is responsible for keeping us in there, much less how to get out.

This brings to mind a story that was told during an episode of my then favorite TV show, *The West Wing*. It goes something like this:

A guy walking down the street falls into a hole. The sides are so steep that it seems impossible to get out, but he tries anyway. He keeps at it hour after hour, slipping back down again on each attempt.

After a while, he realizes that he can see who's walking by if he cranes his neck at the correct angle. A doctor passes by, and the guy shouts up, "Hey, you . . . can you help me out?" The doctor writes a prescription, throws it down the hole, and moves on. Not long afterward, a priest comes along, and the guy yells out, "Father, I'm down in this hole; please, can you help me?" The priest scribbles down a prayer, throws it down the hole, and moves on. Then, to the man's elation, one of his friends walks by. "Joe, it's me! Am I ever glad to see you. Give me some help here, okay?"

At this, the friend jumps into the hole, and our guy says, "Are you stupid? Now we are both down here!"

His friend says, "Yeah, but I've been down here before and I know how to get out."

So, what thrusts us into the hole in the first place? Most people believe that somebody else threw them down there, or that their fall resulted from bad decisions on their part, or that they simply weren't skilled enough to avoid the hole even if they saw it up ahead. So these folks spend much of their life trying to compensate for their own carefully assigned causes. They never realize that the real problem is the paltry self-definition that every human being has accepted—"I am an ego-entity." That is to say, a human being who is separate from all other beings and believes himself to be the author of all of his actions. In fact, the sense of our doership is zealously guarded by a "Do Not Touch" sign that obscures the very place we must look in order to realize that this is not who we are. Often, we spend large portions of our lives repainting the sign. This maintenance falls under the heading "self-mastery."

Another way to say this is that no matter the context of our thoughts, aspirations, and actions, we live in a state of misidentification. This misidentification is a bondage regardless of which mountain we have chosen to climb. It is a function of what the ego assumes itself to be, further fortified by the ego's insistence that its self-definition remain unchallenged. What's more, the sense of security derived from believing that the assumed ego-concept is real propels people in droves to classes, seminars, and workshops to hone and polish this ego that we imagine ourselves to be. This is what I call the drive toward self-mastery.

In saying this, I am not proposing to replace one set of concepts with another; that would merely be redecorating the hole. As it was for our man in the story, only a series of experiential pointers by someone who knows the way out can lead you to an understanding that will disappear the hole. I take it back. That is exactly the wrong way to say it. The reality is that there is no such hole. But you won't know this until those living pointers take root in you. Only then will the shift in ego-definition take you to a new and different felt experience of who you are and, by extension, who and what everything else is.

So what does the life of a hick from the orange groves of Southern California have to do with any of this?

My story begins in the small town of Corona, where I began to suspect that a first glance doesn't reveal the whole picture. Picture a summer day with the temperature hovering around a hundred degrees, and in it place a skinny ten-year-old boy, with freckles that defy his sunburned face, marching down the frontage road of the new freeway in his little hometown. As is usual in this type of weather, he is on his way to the Standard Oil station where a magic metal machine dispenses ice-cold chocolate drinks for five cents. As all inlanders intimately familiar with desert heat can tell you, on such a day you can see the waves of heat rise from the asphalt if you look at exactly the right angle. It's as though another world existed that you can perceive if you tilt your head just so. As the boy looks in wonder at the billows of heat shimmering before his face, the question cannot help but occur to him: How many unseen worlds exist?

If anyone needs to pinpoint the moment when I became a seeker, I guess you could say this was it.

Living in California during the sixties and having a doting grandfather who told me stories about Socrates were part of my early wonder and curiosity about things unknown. A bite of the seeker's bug early in life eventually led me to travels in Peru, India, and many other parts of the world. My journeys, however, were not only to different locations; they also included a career in the corporate financial world, advanced study in academia, years in the ashrams of India, and the convoluted, never-ending drama of relationships, money, and just plain living.

I have spent much of my time and energy bounding after the elusive goal of awakening, which is also called enlightenment. And for the majority of my adult years, I have simultaneously been engaged in climbing the mountain of business. I could have easily done something else, of course, for ultimately one pursuit is the same as any other. There is not a spiritual world out there someplace that is set apart from the corporate—or any other—world. But for a long time, I didn't know this. I can testify that I fell into the seeker's hole, again and again, in whatever territory I was navigating at a given time. After many years, I have discovered that it doesn't matter whether you are seeking awakening, or authentic leadership, or union with God, or peak performance. In order to lead authentically, perform at the very peak, expand awareness, or enter into union with the whole, the bondage of ego-definition must be dissolved.

What it all comes down to is this: Who you really are bubbles up continuously to form the intuition that initiates the seeking. And the seeking that you undertake can indeed eradicate your identification with who you think you are. Moving toward recognizing this truth is a transformational journey in which the "you" that you believe yourself to be will be lost and something entirely new will take its place. "Reclaimed" might be a better term. Either way, it will be vastly different from what you have known before. The secret is: You already are what you are seeking.

No doubt I have gone well beyond what a little boy was able to surmise, looking at those rising heat waves. The discoveries of a lifetime seeker have birthed what is now my life, and I no longer can contain what flows out of my understanding. Thus, I have written this book so that the pointers toward the truth of who you are will give you access to a bigger stage. *Awakened Leadership* can be—if you recognize it to be so—the friend that jumps into your hole and leads you out.

But before you undertake to read a book such as this, let me warn you: It doesn't end in the way you think. To use another metaphor, at the last station on your journey is a platform marked "Perfect Peace," but when you arrive, you notice that what you have believed yourself to be seems to have gone somewhere else. In fact, there is no one on the platform.

That ten-year-old boy was right: All you have to do to see this is tilt your head just so.

Alan E. Shelton
Oceanside, California
July 16, 2011

Introduction

Some time back, I was invited to a conference for about two hundred leadership consultants who wanted to learn and share coaching techniques. At one point, I was asked to demonstrate onstage a one-on-one session with a CEO participant who had volunteered to be a guinea pig. After a twenty-minute demonstration, I was overrun by the enthusiastic response of my fellow coaches. It seems that nobody had ever been exposed to the coaching style that they had just witnessed. True to the corporate world's penchant for reading books, absorbing various approaches, and then attempting to fashion conceptual learning into an on-the-ground coaching method, those who were crowding around me were all eager to know what model I had used. Try as I might, I couldn't answer them; I had not yet developed a way to communicate that I was simply a conduit through which experiential insight funneled itself.

This initiated a deep internal search to prepare a response to such inquiries in the future. What I found was that my life itself had developed into an intuitive container for coaching to take place. The method—if you could call it that—used in the demonstration did not come from any book or model, but rather resided effortlessly in what I had become. It finally occurred to me that the best way to solve this dilemma lay hidden in the stories of my own ego development toward self-mastery and my later attempts to dissolve the boundaries of the self that I was so certain existed. The clue that pointed me in the right direction was something that my grandfather had once said to me: "When scientists find the center of the universe, listen for the sonic boom of all those who are shocked to find that they are not it." He knew that the demand of the ego to occupy that center blinds us to flashes of awakening that could otherwise be seen and absorbed.

My grandfather's simple wisdom was often out of reach for corporate types. But these were my brothers in arms; I was one of them. I wanted to find a way to illustrate this ego-truth in real time and, more important, avoid reducing it to yet another leadership concept. If what I had come to understand couldn't migrate into the experience of those who seemed hungry for this realization, then whatever I told them about it would be useless, despite its veracity.

The relentless seeking I observed in everyone around me, without exception, was evidence that feeling trapped within the boundaries created by the ego is universal. So I began to revisit every stage of my ego development, recalling the stories of my life that intertwined with each one. These tales provided doorways, or pointers, for the executives I coached, other coaches who wanted to expand their own client work, and the spiritual seekers who were attending gatherings in my home. Hearing those stories helped put the tales of their own lives into focus, and soon people were asking where they could find them written down. This book is that place.

Leaders and Seekers Are One and the Same

I have spent most of my life with one foot in the world of business and the other in the domain called spiritual seeking. Like the majority of people who compartmentalize, and then struggle to straddle, two worlds, I watched myself develop within these seemingly separate containers. At a certain point in the arc of my own maturation, it became apparent that all endeavors—whether interior or exterior, individual or relational, spiritual or material—have the same roots and therefore must occupy the same world. My transformational processes and insights ultimately came to nest in the one, single, rooted trunk of experience that had given birth to these seemingly different branches. Spiritual seekers are looking for truth, while corporate types are looking for authenticity.

I have noticed that when it comes to executive leadership, most leaders are looking for a place to be great, whereas spiritual aspirants are seeking a place where they can receive the revelation of ultimate truth. From this vantage point, it became obvious that the separation between achievements in the domain of business and realizations in the spiritual realm is artificial. These pursuits are one and the same.

If it is held that the entirety of the human drama, corporate or otherwise, is simply a stage for the development and expansion of its participants, then it must be true that managing corporate transactions offers the same platform for evolving consciousness as anything else can. Conversely, what has traditionally been considered to be the exclusive domain of the seeker extends beyond the walls of ashrams and the gathering rooms of the great teachers and gurus. Passionate seeking—and total commitment—is not the monopoly of any one group. Corporate experience is as real and authentic as that of the philosopher-king. And the potential for living in what is known as the awakened state is equally present in every domain of life.

It soon became clear that I am far from alone in viewing reality from this perspective. The larger world is developing a hunger for the same kind of realization and expansion that, until recently, was the province of only gurus and sages. And the participants in the corporatization of our global economy have begun to demand nothing less than a platform for their own transformation. While the mainstream press brands anything corporate as the handiwork of the Dark Side, that perception could not be further from the truth. The corporate landscape is teeming with the demand for offerings in personal development and consciously responsible leadership. Where these are made available, you will find today's best executives. These men and women have a keen ear for identifying opportunities to expand through their own personal journey and, at the same time, to develop traits that will facilitate successful outcomes in business. Much as I do, they live with relish every corporate moment. They do not want the lifeblood of their passion marginalized or diluted as though it were of a lesser value.

For corporate leadership to be true leadership, it must result in—and derive from—the felt experience of the leader himself. This requires that the tools and devices for personal clarity track side by side with those of leadership development. A leader with a clear vision of himself extends this capacity to see to all who follow him. So we must trace the route all the way back to the original misidentification with the ego-self that we absorbed when we were very young and which blurs our sight today. The personal journey, inseparable from the leader's quest, makes awakening the lifework of those who pursue either goal. When we as leaders are in the awakened state, we find ourselves being lived perfectly in the realm where we belong. Only this can be properly called Awakened Leadership.

If you have picked up this book, you are most likely clamoring for a directly perceivable experience of truth that will match your passion. You don't need another directory of models, maps, and concepts, because you know by now that the map isn't the territory. So who can launch you into that territory and then help you explore it in your own shoes? You know in your bones that personal growth is available right now, and right where you stand, but what can take you beyond canned transformational processes? If these are your questions, then what you are now facing is a decision about whether you are going to leap into the unknown.

Awakened Leadership has been written for you.

Awakening Belongs to Experience

The difference between this and most other leadership books lies in the recognition that leadership concepts must be birthed from within the truth of experience, not the other way around. Nowhere is this more important than when it comes to what is known as awakening and Awakened Leadership. Simply put, the term "awakening" is a placeholder for the arising of the internal, felt sense that your actions seamlessly reside in who you really are and move in a perfect flow.

The words in this book can convey a conceptual sense of the awakened state, but any intellectual understanding that you may glimpse is just a stop along the way. Moments of direct insight into your own experience provide some sweet relief from the limitations of meanings derived from cognitive thought, but you are not meant to rest there for long either. The function of understanding and insight is to point you to the next stop, which is beyond either of these: the actual experience of awakening. *Awakening is the experience to which all of these concepts simply point.*

When you have made the move from conceptual understanding all the way to your lived experience of wholeness, it is similar to feeling the sudden warmth on your upturned face when the sun breaks through after a spate of cold, overcast days. That's when the soundtrack of all your thoughts and actions will resonate in perfect pitch with your true self. This moment of awakening can then be expanded to become the ground of all/your experience.

The awakened state is not reached with an instruction manual in hand. I wrote this book because my experience as both a leader and a seeker has demonstrated the value of hearing stories and absorbing concepts that serve as pointers within the territory that must be walked on the journey of awakening. My aim in telling the stories of my life is not to provide you with new and interesting tales to tell your associates and friends. Nor is it possible for my stories to create a specific pathway for your life, either personally or professionally. These tales are intended to shed light on the stages of human expansion and development and the myriad challenges that confront the dedicated seeker along the way. I use them to illustrate ego development and its maturity into awakening. Consider them as opportunities to inhabit your own stories so that the learning you extract from them will advise you on your journey. They will invite you to dig through your life and discover where your own stories have led you thus far, so that you can begin to intuit where they may want to take you next.

Put Your Feet on the Path

To make the material in this book accessible to all types of readers, whatever their particular style of learning, a number of different approaches are used. In addition to my personal stories, teaching anecdotes from Zen and Sufi sources, stories heard on TV shows, and even song lyrics and children's tales, open up various access points. The first twelve chapters highlight my personal stories. Chapters 13 through 16 focus on four specific areas—ego-definition, presence, service, and relationships—illustrating how awakening moments play out in each of these arenas. Chapter 17 describes the coaching process as a device for awakening, and chapter 18, the final chapter, offers pointers that can become doorways to the awakened state. All of these access points lead to the same outcome.

As you read through this book, you will undoubtedly encounter ideas and concepts that are foreign or uncomfortable. Your first response might be confusion, upset, or even anger that I do not make them clearer. My intent is to nudge you from concept into experience. Experience itself is an unknown. We simply can't predict what will happen when we enter into any experience. The ego, which always demands solid ground to stand on, doesn't like the unknown and will push it away with all its strength. But I want you to make friends with it. Let yourself be confused by or frustrated with concepts that are new and foreign. Wait. Allow the experiences they bring into your life and see what happens. The movement into your own awakening experience will always be a foray into the unknown.

The indicators along the pathway will become obvious as you read this book. But where does the journey begin for *you*?

Many years ago, at the age of eighteen, I read a book by Stephen Covey entitled *Spiritual Roots of Human Relations*. I was struck by his metaphoric comparison of human development to the seven days of Creation by divine fiat. Covey insisted that the first step in all personal development is to make a ruthless assessment of where you are on your journey. This is the place from which you must begin. That is to say, if you are in the second day of your own creation but pretending to be in the fourth, this will only produce insurmountable obstacles to your progress. Starting where you are is direct and real. It will infuse the rest of the process with a sense of traction, informing you that there is no masking or pretense.

And so my invitation to you is to imagine a reality in which you arise as the highest form of awareness, no matter where you are in any given moment or what you are doing. No longer will it be necessary to seek out diagrams and models that are a distant reflection of another's journey. You will be effortlessly reflected into every situation in a way that only you can be. Much like the gurus and sages who look to their own experience and report out to those that surround them, you too can expand into that perfect space and become the invitation to others to join you there. That is the promise of this book and the possibility contained within. *Awakened Leadership* is my heartfelt gift pointing to that outcome.

The Red Hatchet

After I had struggled for some time to write something about myself that might convey the experience of awakening that occurred in the life of Alan, my editor prodded me with the following comment. "Alan," she said, "just throw them in the water." This was both surprising and interesting, for if you had followed the span of my lifetime, you would know that it has been—if anything—one experience after another of jumping into the water with no thought whatsoever.

Early case in point: I was in second grade in the city of Provo, Utah, and my father was attending college after his stint in the Navy. As he neared graduation, my parents were getting our little family ready to move to California, where Dad was going to take his first job. I was part of a Cub Scout troop at the time and none too happy about the idea of being torn away from it—especially not right then, for reasons that will become clear. The news of our upcoming departure was delivered one evening after I got home from a troop meeting. I hadn't been sent upstairs to change, so I sat slumped in one of the chairs around the kitchen table and waited for dinner—probably venison with potatoes, my father's favorite and thus the family standard.

At all of eight years old, I had already developed, like many boys my age, the ability to have clothing hang off my skinny frame as though it were a crumpled flag. It could be said that my Scout uniform looked more like the brave banner of Francis Scott Key, which, although tattered and riddled with holes, was found to be still there. Some of the niceties of life, such as tidy dress habits, were ignored by most of us in the Cub den in favor of important boy escapades. A world of wonder moved through our Cub Scout souls, and we wasted nary an extra minute doing any one thing, for the next big adventure was always moving in to take the last one's place. In the excitement of purloining apples, splashing our way through a pond in pursuit of bugs skating on the surface, and the like, the way our clothing looked was the least of our concerns.

The timing of my father's announcement couldn't have been worse. At the meeting that evening, I had learned that our troop would be selling boxes of chocolate. I couldn't have cared less about selling chocolate, except for the one fact that turned the moment on its head: It was a contest, and the Cub Scout who sold the most boxes would win a red hatchet. My first memory of my boy world coming to a complete stop is encapsulated in the moment when I heard this. The prospect of winning that red hatchet so caught my imagination that nothing that had happened before, and nothing that would happen after, could compete with it. I'm not sure that at any time in my life, the desire to secure an outcome has been stronger than it was in the prepubescent boy who had to have that hatchet. Treating this contest as merely the next adventure was out of the question; I somehow knew this with no prior experience of formal competition. The race was on, and I needed to stop everything else and deliver.

There was one big problem: The contest deadline was a week after our family was scheduled to leave town.

Now my father and I never had much to share with each other; in fact, we most often lived in mutual suspicion and anger. But his natural talent for coming up with solutions to apparently unsolvable dilemmas won out over his general disinclination to help make things work better for his son. In order to understand the dimensions of the situation, it's important to know that the boxes of chocolate came twelve to a case and that the winner of the last candy-selling contest had sold twelve cases. That's 144 boxes, which is a lot of chocolate. My dad pointed out that if I could outsell everyone else by enough boxes before we left, it was highly unlikely that the result of the contest would be questioned, even a week before the deadline. I took this to mean that there would be no doubt in anyone's mind that I had won. His solution leaped larger than life into my imagination. There was a way to get that hatchet!

In that moment, everything else that had been of interest to me was ushered off the stage, seemingly by itself. I felt heat bubbling up in my body; it was a call to action, a challenge to make that solution real. From that point on, the forced march to win the prize could arguably have been called a compulsion. But that drive was also a surrender, a surrender to the unquenchable call to win, which would become the M.O. that would anchor me—and haunt me—throughout most of my life.

To add to the drama, we were scheduled to leave in December, and Provo was already in the midst of one of the wettest winters it had seen. This meant having to trudge from door to door through the snow and slush to sell my chocolate. I would come home from school and, with barely a word to my mother, grab a snack and launch off with my boxes. I remember the look of weary exasperation on her face when she finally would find me after driving around in the dark for hours. You see, that red hatchet had no sense of whether I was selling chocolates in the light of day or the dark of night. To this young boy, the setting of the sun had no meaning.

As it turns out, I was able to sell a fair amount of chocolate. In fact, by the time I was done, I had sold 135 cases. Now for those of you without a calculator at hand, that amounts to 1,620 boxes of chocolate. I sold my last box on a Friday afternoon, three weeks after the contest had opened. My pack meeting the following evening would be my last before leaving for California.

The next day dragged on interminably.

When I got to the meeting, I couldn't do much besides fidget and look around. When were they going to say something about my contest? Toward the end of a tortured hour and a half, Dan, our pack leader, finally stood up to give an update.

My pack leader was a man who had taken a liking to me and had encouraged me often, and he knew that I had worked hard selling my chocolates. Dan gave the usual speech about good sportsmanship as I, alongside my dozen and a half sales buddies, squirmed on one of those metal folding chairs so common in multipurpose rooms. I did my best to look interested, and settled for watching his face. He was trying to look stern, but then I noticed something else in his eyes. I sensed that my moment had come.

Dan shifted his weight, cleared his throat, and spoke out in his clear voice. "The boy who is second in the running in our contest has sold 12 cases so far. And our top seller"—he paused briefly and then turned his head to look directly at me—"has sold . . . 135 cases. Because the difference is so large, and he is leaving tomorrow, we are going to award the red hatchet to Alan."

Before I had a chance to absorb this, the father of the second-place boy jumped up. "But there's still a week to go. It's possible that my boy can catch up with him."

Every child, boy or girl, knows the sound of that voice—the voice of an adult who speaks from a set of rules rather than the spirit of the moment. It is also the silent sound of a promise dropping from the heart of a small child into the pit of his stomach. In the name of an ideal that has no meaning, this voice deflates the burst of joy that comes naturally to every human being who knows that he has triumphed and deserves to win.

Absurd as his protest was, you can imagine that I was utterly crushed. However, my pack leader said quietly but firmly, "We are going to award the red hatchet to Alan, and if your son catches up with him in the next week, I will personally buy him one as well."

By that point in my life, I had already heard about the wisdom of King Solomon. I didn't make the connection at the time, but Dan had proved to be my living Solomon. In front of a group of kids who looked to him to protect them, this wise and caring man had delivered a judgment that honored common sense and the tenacity of a little boy rather than rules that made a claim to fairness but, instead, stole the truth.

The following morning, I was assigned the job of helping my dad pack our car. I had slept all night clutching my hatchet, waking up constantly to assure myself that it still was mine, and now I was reluctant to put it down even for a few minutes. My dad finally convinced me that it wouldn't go anywhere if I let him put it on the dashboard, where it would be visible at all times.

The memory of leaving Provo in our pastel-green 1953 Pontiac with my prize on my lap is one of the happiest of my entire childhood. Of all of the things I have ever owned, that little red hatchet is my favorite, to this day.

You might be asking yourself, "What bearing does this story have on the journey of awakening?" Oh, but you will see that at every significant event in my life, I have jumped in the water or scrambled up the mountain. I suspect I have always felt that there is a red hatchet at the bottom of every lake or on the peak of every mountain I come across. And I didn't approach my spiritual pilgrimage any differently.

And so it was that in this warrior child, the urge arose to conquer everything that life would deliver in front of his little face. As he advanced in years, society would relentlessly deliver layer after layer of shoulds, woulds, and coulds. But the initial surge of total response that was now wired into that child would emerge in the face of any challenge and eventually take him into worlds that his future corporate guardians could not conceive of.

From their perspective, that Cub-Scout-turned-CEO belonged on the mountaintop of Corporate America with his red hatchet. Indeed, he managed to get there quite easily, and had no qualms about swinging around that hatchet above his head. But what they saw was a man who hadn't arrived by way of the rules, and that bothered the hell out of them. In rejecting his explorations, they rejected him, with the taut accusation that he was living a life hopelessly compromised. They refused to believe that the journey of the heart could be woven into the structured life of an achiever bent on meeting the most daunting challenges. So they spoke about him in the same voice as the father in that pack meeting, agreeing with one another that he was wasting his life in the pursuit of a crazy dream. They shook their heads and walked away, feeling sorry for the *wunderkind* who, they said, had ended up as a misused talent.

It would be in an arena far different from the business world where full-throttled passion as my baseline response to life was recognized by someone who could put it into the proper context for me. It took another man like Solomon—in this case, one who had scaled mountains similar to the ones I knew so well—to bring it all together. Years later, in October 2005, I would find myself in a living room in Mumbai (Bombay), India, in the presence of a man whose wisdom honored not only the achievement of a mountain climbed but also a boundless spirit that only a seeker's heart can hold. His name was Ramesh Balsekar.

I had the custom of going at nine o'clock every morning to Ramesh's satsang, the ancient tradition of seekers gathering in the presence of an awakened sage. I would then return in the afternoon when he was available and we would sit and talk about our favorite man-topics. He was a graduate of the London School of Economics and a former CEO of the Bank of India, so we would often swap business stories, as businessmen do. One warm afternoon, Ramesh stopped in the middle of a conversation and, looking at me with those piercing eyes of his, said, "Alan, do you remember when I said that Albert Einstein was just the right body-mind to transmit the theory of relativity?"

I did remember, because it's one of my favorite examples of how truth would come through him and light up the room. Ramesh used the term "body-mind" rather than "I" or "you" to remind us not to identify with our body or our ego. When Ramesh talked about the body-mind, he would often point out that Albert Einstein was the only vessel that had the circuitry to receive and be lived by manifestation such that the theory of relativity could have been delivered to mankind. Ramesh used this example so that his followers would understand that they are not doers, nor are they the authors of their own lives; they are tools of manifestation for the delivery of whatever Existence makes happen through them. The idea that Einstein was the author of the theory of relativity is an illusion. Though he was perfectly suited for the job, he was simply a part of the discovery of what is true about energy, mass, and light. That theory was not a product of self-mastery but rather of Source itself.

On this particular day, Ramesh felt to tell me that I, as another specially designed transmitter—as we all are—reminded him in some way of Albert Einstein. And then he said, "Alan, you are the receptacle and deliverer of passion. In fact, when I speak with you, it often surprises me that someone with your capacity for passion could ever be attracted to an understanding that takes the passion out of the hands of the supposed author of his own activity. Usually, folks of your ilk guard their passion like a king's treasure."

From that day on, it was our little secret, and a source of humor, that passion arises most often and most closely intertwined with the sense of being identified with the ego-self. This leads to the obvious question: How can a person who is a container of passion follow the road of a living understanding that embodies disidentification from the ego? And to its corollary: How do we live embraced in the bosom of overwhelming passion and, at the same time, understand that passion is not a possession. And that we neither author nor direct the outcome of that energy?

In one sense, these inquiries, and the passion behind them, were no different for the adult Alan than the question that arose in his eight-year-old self of how to win a red hatchet. In their more sophisticated form, however, these sorts of questions will not be encountered until one enters the domain of mature seekers of truth. I raise them here as living pointers to unknown experiences that one may encounter along the way, and as a means to tease out new possibilities in the mind of a reader.

Nobody comes into this world knowing what his path is going to look like. Each child is given—small piece by small piece—only a fragmented picture of how things fit together. Before the play begins, he waits in the wings to be ushered onstage. Once the script starts to roll, he will soon be required—no matter what his natural gifts may be—to encounter his own unbridled energy. Most of the other actors in his life will be all too happy to channel him into the straitjacket experience of being conditioned. It is here that all egos begin their development, thrown without warning into conflicting influences: On one side are the energies that naturally surge through a little child, and on the other is the requirement that they be delivered according to society's notions of appropriate behavior, in acceptable installments. It was no different for me.

This societal demand forms the basis of the concept that individuals can be developed into masters of their own affairs. But the fact that the mind can think about or conceive of something does not make it possible. As we will discover, self-mastery is one of those concepts that seduce all of us with a promise that can never be fulfilled.

2 Grandpa's Enchanted Kingdom

I am sure that in every life you can find clues to why certain outcomes emerge. My life was a mixture of two unique variables: The first was an intellectual and energetic nesting that I enjoyed from my early days. The second was a cumbersome and suffocating religious structure full of rules. What is interesting is that when I was embedded in religious structures, I responded with all the strength and energy that I possessed. I don't believe that there is anything in my life that I have not tested or tried to the fullest extent, out of a deep desire to know if something worthwhile lies at the end. But I am already digressing. First, the happy years in the kingdom of my grandfather.

I was born in 1953 into a typical intellectual Northern California family. My grandfather was a distinguished financial officer in the automobile business, having graduated from a respected San Francisco university. My mother graduated from high school a year early and was headed on a scholarship to another prestigious college. During the first semester, however, the family tragedy occurred. My mom, only seventeen years old, became pregnant. You can imagine that an unmarried woman with a small child was not the best fit with the status-conscious San Francisco social scene of that era. Shortly after I was born, however, my grandfather had the opportunity to be a founding partner in the first Pontiac dealership in the Southern California community of San Diego. So when I was eighteen months old, my grandparents, my mother, my aunt (who is a year and a half older than I am and was more like a sister), my uncle, and I all moved to Southern California.

My mother and I lived in a little apartment over the garage of a large and beautiful house that my grandparents occupied with my aunt and uncle. To this day, it is common to see these Spanish-style, white-plaster and red-tile homes overlooking the ocean from the hillsides of San Diego. To a little boy who loved to paint fences and play in the garden, it was a magical paradise.

My grandfather, in essence, was my father, and was at the point in life where he relished the opportunity to have a little boy accompany him in pretty much all he did outside of work. I used to wait like a puppy dog for Grandpa to return home each day from the dealership. And it seemed to me that Grandpa did all he could to make sure that he was there to return that feeling. It was from this man that I received the unmistakable, unique experience of being completely held. As it is with most of my childhood memories, the sense of those moments is pure and singular. So when I say that my grandfather held me, I mean that I had the experience of orbiting in who he was, held securely in place as all grandson planets should be. It wasn't until many years later, when I found my first master, Osho, that I rediscovered this feeling.

I often relive memories from this time, many of them of my grandmother, such as watching a big gob of chocolate ice cream slide down Grandma's back when she braked suddenly, leaving me holding an empty cone; and being left accidentally at the grocery store and feasting with the owner on goodies that he had selected for us to enjoy. I still can see the puzzled look on my grandmother's face as a shower of dollar bills landed and fluttered against the windshield. Puzzled, that is, until she turned and saw her eldest grandson digging into her purse and gleefully flinging bills out the copilot window and people running over to scoop them up. And, of course, the famous scene of me scarfing down chocolate birthday cake on Grandma's white satin bedspread on the day I turned two. All of these adventures took place in the rarified, living air that my grandfather wove around his entire family.

Being his oldest grandson was probably the best job that anybody could possibly have. And I got it with no interview or qualifications. I sat next to my grandfather at every meal. He, being a man who demanded the best, never ate anything but the finest and purest food. Forget Imperial Margarine and Miracle Whip—it was only real butter and real mayonnaise for us. But the best part was that every night, Grandpa would take me on his knee and tell me stories that nobody else in the family seemed to care about. It was from him that I learned about a philosopher whose name was Socrates. I was a verbally active child, so I had thousands of questions, and I received Grandpa's support to ask every single one of them. Due to my incessant habit, he told me how the little boys who hung around Socrates would ask the same questions. It wasn't until years later that I realized that his interlocutors were probably much older than the four-year-old in San Diego. Nonetheless, not only did my grandpa respond every time, he would also add, "Do you think that answer is right, Alan?" He would always encourage me to turn over every idea and look under it, like a prospector searching for that elusive gold nugget.

You see, my grandfather was a short, quiet man with a razor-sharp gaze that took in more than most people ever notice. That natural ability, coupled with the never-ending patience to talk with his young grandchild, was the great delight of my childhood. To his dying day, one of our favorite conversations was about an interchange that took place when I was five, after he had read "The Emperor's New Clothes" to me.

GRANDPA: Alan, why do you think that little boy told everyone that the emperor in the parade was wearing nothing?

ALAN: Grandpa, how could he help himself? The emperor didn't have anything on.

GRANDPA: So why do you think everybody was surprised when the boy said that?

ALAN: They must've been thinking something else.

GRANDPA: Well, what were they thinking?

ALAN: Umm . . . they must have been thinking that he had clothes on, when it's clear that he really didn't.

GRANDPA: Alan, always remember that adults think a lot of things like that.

ALAN: But Grandpa, why do they have to do that when they can just see that there are no clothes?

GRANDPA: Because adults are always much happier when they agree with each other rather than seeing the parade that's passing in front of their face.

A twinkle in the eye and a faint smile always passed between us on these occasions. Everything in our world was fair game for whatever poking and prodding we might want to do. I am sure that nobody but me knew that the man who ran the Pontiac dealership in town was involved in such conversations, which somehow made them "just ours."

I could tell you story after story—in fact, it's remarkable that a man my age has such distinct memories from so long ago. But what's important is that the seed-desire to seek the deepest possible truth was planted in my heart during this time. It's not that my grandpa demanded it; the two of us simply shared an undeniable and unquenchable need to look into things and understand them.

As long as Grandpa was present to keep tending the rich soil that this seed inhabited, all was well. Unfortunately, as you will see, my relentless questioning was soon to collide with a world that claimed it fostered such searching but certainly did not. For the world of adults does not contain anywhere near enough grandfathers who will encourage a young boy to ask the searing questions that have to be asked if he is to grow into the warrior-man nested within. And practically no one will support him when he comes into young manhood, when the questions will burn even more brightly in him.

For many young doers, the path to an adult future in which the essence of the intuitive and experiential can flower is obscured. Instead, the collective power of groupthink, which insists that the clothes are on the king when in fact they are not, has come to represent the highest point in our ascent. Fortunately, some of us finally manage to find the sleeping giants of "here" and "now" that gift to us an authenticity that can never be displaced. But often it takes setting out on a journey to get there.

Most psychologists agree that the ego begins to develop at the age of two or two and a half. That's when a child learns that, rather than being an indistinguishable part of all that is, she is a self-contained entity with her own identity. Ramesh Balsekar often referred to this as "entification." Many believe that the later awakening of a body-mind into full consciousness is simply a return to the time of childhood before that identification with a separate self occurs. But this is not the case. One's awakening is actually a return to the childlike energy of the felt sense of being all that is—but with the adult, developed intellect as part of the package. The bridge back to that pure consciousness that was all but buried by adult intellect consists of seeing through those so-called mature concepts, which cling like mud to a shingle, and into the unknown underneath. It is into this unknown—beyond self-mastery as it is commonly understood—that we must go. Only there can direct experience outside the conceptual awaken and begin to accompany us, like our own personal Merlin, on our life journey.

In fact, Ramesh held that it is through concept itself that one eliminates a prior held and felt concept. He called this "a living understanding." Ramana Maharshi, one of the great Indian saints and sages of the twentieth century, used to say that concepts are like thorns: You use one to dig out the other and then you throw them both away, so that the direct experience of truth that is beyond both can naturally arise.

And so it was that the first living understanding that came to define Alan was the one developed in the nest of my grandfather. Lest anyone have the question, the women in my family were an undeniably potent influence as well. My grandmother and my mother were hatched out of the same type of egg. These were give-no-quarter and take-no-nonsense women. It was from them that I learned how to exercise power in life as I knew it. It was the kind of full-throttled power that sage women have wielded down the ages and understand well, a power that invariably accomplishes its unapologetic purpose. But it always does so with an eye to making sure that what is important is left intact, so that the web of life has a resting place from which to regenerate itself.

Later on in life, when people would ask me about my mother or my grandmother, I would say, "They were like oncoming freight trains. The secret of learning how to deal with either of them was to recognize when and how to get off the tracks." I found out early on that my mother and I didn't necessarily have the same interests, so most of the time it was expedient, and not difficult, to move off the tracks and avoid a collision. But you will see how their style of power crops up in my own behaviors later in life. For, much like them, I have never been able to separate the exercise of power from the service of love—even if clumsily expressed—to those in my life.

Welcome to Hell

Perhaps you have heard the story about an Indian king who asked an old sage to advise him on a most urgent matter. It seems that the mighty army of a neighboring kingdom, led by the king's most feared enemy, was threatening to attack. The sage listened in silence to the anxious monarch, and then promised to give him a secret that would help him at the very moment when it was absolutely needed. And so, the next day, he handed the king a ring, inside of which the sage had ordered the royal jeweler to engrave a message. Under no circumstance was the king to look at the message before the situation required it. The king was dubious, but the sage would say no more.

A fierce battle shortly ensued, and the king's adversary met with almost immediate success. The king's troops were badly outnumbered, and he realized that he would easily be caught and killed unless he made a hasty retreat from the battlefield and hid in the forest nearby. He rode hard, the pounding of hooves behind him growing louder as the enemy horsemen gained on him. In the heightened fear of the moment, he assumed that the time was at hand. Almost completely spent and out of breath, he turned into a glade of trees, pulled the ring off his finger, and read the words inscribed inside:

THIS TOO SHALL PASS

In one of those inexplicable turns of fate, it seems that the pursuing horsemen were not able to find the king among the trees; confused, they retreated, and the king was able to make a hasty escape. The story goes that later that day, this king was able to regather his forces and make a heroic comeback, thereby retaining his kingdom. Of course, such a victory demanded a parade through the gates back into his city. As the king, in great delight, received the adoration of all his countrymen in the city square, he noticed the sage standing along the parade route. As he bent down to thank the old man, he heard him say, "*Now* is the time to read the message in your ring."

Living with my grandparents and mother in the magical circumstances I have described to you, I couldn't imagine that life could get much better. And I certainly never imagined that it could get worse. But, as you might guess, I was wrong, and that time did pass. My mother was a fairly attractive woman living in a city full of young military men, and the inevitable happened. When I was on the tail end of four years old, my mother met the man I would know as my father. Soon after the young couple met—my father was twenty—they decided to get married, and we went to live with him on the Navy base. This was a turbulent period; amidst the difficulties of forging a new relationship, my mother discovered that she was pregnant with my brother Ray.

My father had grown up in a small southern Utah town. He was the son of an alcoholic, and his mother had died just about the time he met my mother. The men in their town made their living principally by working in uranium mines in southern Utah and Nevada, and I am sure that my father saw enlisting in the Navy as a better opportunity than spending a lifetime as a miner. So he joined up, became a chief petty officer, and served in the Korean War. Dad was a quiet, reserved, and angry man. As is not unusual for males of this type, it was a difficult task to assume the care of a persistent, incessantly questioning child who did not know his place. This was not a man who trafficked much in talk. The verbal part of our relationship extended only as far as a few well-placed orders, none of which required a child's input. Disobedience led to the discipline that needed no words. Thus it was inevitable that an instant and lifelong wariness arose between us. If I was the mouse and he was the cat, I was determined to become a faster mouse.

Sometime during the first year of their marriage, we got word that my father was soon to be discharged from the Navy. With the G.I. Bill at his back, he was able to apply to Brigham Young University in Provo, where he was accepted. I remember well the day that we packed up our old Pontiac and headed out across the desert to move to a new place where my father could get an education. I was still only five years old, and leaving my grandfather held a terror that I have never forgotten. Perhaps that is why, to this day, I cannot even remember saying good-bye to him.

The next two years initiated the intensive conditioning phase of my life. I also had a lot of fun, since it was the first time I had ever experienced winter and seen snow. But even my greatest adventures were overshadowed by a constant state of being in survival. It seemed that I was always looking over my shoulder, afraid of the unknown and unpleasant at the hands of both my family and my new environment.

Shortly after we arrived, my parents were able to buy a small brick house that was some five blocks from the elementary school where I would enter my kindergarten year. When I remember that house, the image of the basement with its walls of never-ending knotty pine is especially vivid. It was in this setting that I had my first encounters with physical violence. Here, for infractions that were small, large, or fabricated, my father would wield his wide black cowboy belt, lashing out at my brother and me who, in short order, would be rolling around helplessly in the corner. If Dad was especially angry, he would use the other end of the belt. Since I was older and bigger than my brother, I would do what was necessary to divert the blows in my direction when I thought that Ray would be the main target of my dad's wrath. I just assumed that this is what big brothers do.

I am sure that each time this occurred, it must have been a loud affair with a lot of crying and expressions of pain. But to be honest, when I remember these scenes, I hear no sound. I'm just standing, outraged, fierce, and promising with all the intensity that is in me that someday I will set all of this right.

I often wondered why my mother who, up to this point in my life, had seemed to shield me from most everything that could harm me, suddenly came up missing. It was as if everything I had come to rely upon had suddenly been yanked from my hands. My grandpa, who surely would have found a way to prevent this horror, was a million miles away in California. That bubble of protection that I assumed would always be there . . . gone. And my mom, who had been as much my companion and friend as my mother, seemed to ignore this need of mine.

As I review those years, I am sure that my mother could not bear to think about what the future would hold, were her second relationship to end in the same way as her first. And so I suspect that I became the sacrifice such that this would not happen again. It is true that this later insight led to an adult understanding that released a lot of the pain I had to feel during my inner transformation process. However, the heartache that I felt as a boy who was not being protected by his mother would never be forgotten.

All of this internal turbulence drove me to look outward for relief. Sensitive child that I was, I had to find a way to deflect the incoming arrows in this new situation. I soon learned how to take my beloved gift of conversation that I shared with my grandfather and mold it into a shield that I could use as protection. But the first thing I discovered when we moved to Provo was that I was an outsider, that is, someone who had not grown up in the neighborhood and had recently arrived from California, to boot. Several of the neighborhood kids decided that they would gang up on this new boy and see what made him tick. Their approach was to chase me home from school for all five blocks to let me know who was in charge.

I remember the races that were held at the end of my first year for all the students in the first, second and third grades. I won the foot race not only for the first graders but also for all three grades combined. I attribute that to the fact that I was chased every day for the first year I attended that school. I was never caught by those kids. No one ever caught up with me in a race either. But I later found out that I was not the fleetest of runners, so I can only surmise that I performed at an Olympic standard solely when being chased by large groups of menacing boys.

Whether it was the turbulence of the times or the specter of raising two young, healthy boys, my mother decided that a religious presence was needed in our lives. As the story is told in our family, she went to my father and asked him which religion they should choose for themselves and for raising their two young sons. My father responded, "I really don't care, as long as it's not the Catholic Church." Up to the time of my father's entry into our family, we had been Catholic, but we were not religious. I remember my grandpa often saying that he was agnostic. A notion of a God was never necessary for him to be the man that he was. His religious sense was beautifully conveyed through his essence.

Knowing that my father had been raised in southern Utah and was ostensibly a Mormon, my mother decided to take lessons from some Mormon missionaries. My earliest memories of this time include young men wearing ties riding their bicycles up to the house and engaging my mother in polite but fervent conversation about some fellow named Joseph Smith. How was I to know that someday I too would emerge into the street with one of those well-ironed white shirts draped from my nineteen-year-old frame?

It was but a short time later that my mother decided to be baptized into the Mormon Church. Like most first-generation converts, my mother took her conversion seriously and with such gusto that she could only be described as a zealot. No amount of energy was spared in attempting to bring her two boys into the fold. But I'd already had a taste of something far different than any structured religion could deliver. (It is to her credit that, although she stuck to her own beliefs, for most of my life my mom was able to support whatever I was doing. I can remember all the moments when she looked me in the eyes and said, "Alan, I know this is the right thing for you.")

The most confusing part of my early existence in Provo was the new relationship that the family was forming with the Mormon Church. Sundays had been a time for watching TV or digging holes in the garden.

Now, every single week, Sunday was given over to a series of tedious church meetings that ate up the entire day. The first began at seven thirty in the morning and ran until nine, followed by Sunday school from ten o'clock till noon. After the family meal, another meeting started at five. When I was nineteen, a church newsletter article, aptly entitled "Primary Headache Goes on Mission," described me as follows: "Alan Shelton left the mission home in Salt Lake City to enter the language-training mission in Provo before leaving for Peru. His mother paid an interesting tribute to the Sunday school teacher who made it her goal for the year to get Alan to sit on the chair and not under it."[1]

Whether she was successful or not isn't the point of the story. What was accomplished in this segment of my conditioning left me with an indelible distaste for attending church. Nevertheless, my natural hunger for new and unknown experiences often led me to check out any other kind of religious service that drew my interest or piqued my curiosity.

When I give satsang, I often use metaphors to illustrate a point. One of my favorites is the process of learning to drive a car. I'm sure that anyone who drives will remember the first time you undertook making an automobile move along a busy street. When you got into the car, the first thing you might have been struck by was the bewildering number of buttons, mirrors, dials, sticks, and pedals. There were so many items and so many actions that you had to know about in order to drive properly, that it was probably quite daunting. Fast-forward a couple of weeks, however, and there you are—jumping into your car, jamming the key in the ignition, throwing the transmission into reverse, peering over your shoulder, and then entering into traffic in forward gear. . . all the while trying to locate your favorite radio station. What happened between the first time you drove the car and the scene a fortnight later is that you were conditioned. All the trivial detail you had to train yourself to remember descended into the basement of your subconscious. Once this happened, you never again needed to summon up all the details from your mind, unless you planned to fly to some other part of the world where they drive on the wrong side of the road, or some other strange thing.

My life in Utah was a learning of this kind, but in this case, I was being taught a whole new way to be. I learned that I needed to be tough to survive. I learned that I needed to use my mental faculties to compete with those around me. And slowly, that sensitive little boy who used to listen to his grandfather with such yearning began to disappear. In my teenage years, a song sung by Peter, Paul, and Mary called "Puff, the Magic Dragon" became very popular. I couldn't help but feel, even at that time, that this song accurately described the journey of my early life.

> *Puff, the magic dragon, lived by the sea*
> *And frolicked in the autumn mist in a land called Honah Lee*
> *Little Jackie Paper loved that rascal Puff*
> *And brought him strings and sealing wax and other fancy stuff.*
>
> *Oh, Puff, the magic dragon, lived by the sea*
> *And frolicked in the autumn mist in a land called Honah Lee.*
>
> *Together they would travel on a boat with billowed sail*
> *Jackie kept a lookout perched on Puff's gigantic tail*
> *Noble kings and princes would bow whene'er they came*
> *Pirate ships would lower their flag when Puff roared out his name.*
>
> *A dragon lives forever, but not so little boys*
> *Painted wings and giant rings make way for other toys.*
> *One grey night it happened, Jackie Paper came no more*
> *And Puff, that mighty dragon, he ceased his fearless roar.*
>
> *His head was bent in sorrow, green scales fell like rain*
> *Puff no longer went to play along the cherry lane.*
> *Without his life-long friend, Puff could not be brave*
> *So Puff, that mighty dragon, sadly slipped into his cave.*
>
> *Oh, Puff, the magic dragon, lived by the sea*
> *And frolicked in the autumn mist in a land called Honah Lee.*

Puff, the magic dragon, lived by the sea
And frolicked in the autumn mist in a land called Honah Lee.

Whenever I hear these words, I always feel the sense of having once lived in a magic kingdom that is well remembered but now lost in the mist of a childhood viewed from a far distance, never to be touched again.

4 The Desert Years

A favorite story of mine is one of the many told about a humorous character believed to have lived in the Middle Ages—a Sufi mystic and philosopher by the name of Mullah Nasruddin. It seems that one day the mullah lost the key to his house, and he decided to call all his friends together so that they could engage in a mass search for it. When they all gathered, he led them to the busiest of all the local markets. In one of the most densely trafficked areas, he got down on his hands and knees and began to search in every corner for the key. The others diligently followed suit until, finally, one of his friends looked up and asked, "Mullah, is this where you lost your key?"

"No," the mullah immediately replied, "but I thought this would be the best place to look because it is so well lit."

In this little tale, we can easily see the conflict between intellectual conditioning and common sense. However, in the development of self-mastery, we continually take on ideas that become unconscious elements in our approach to everyday activity. In the mullah's case, the concept that a search should take place in the most well illuminated location became a conditioned response that overrode the obvious fact that he and his friends should do their looking where the item was actually lost.

In observing how the conditioning of the body-mind proceeds in most human beings, it seems to me that the crossroads where experience and developed intellect meet is a natural point of congestion. The tension that arises at that juncture must be worked out in the teenage years for an individual to function at a reasonable level of integration.

This was exactly the case for me and, because I was born in 1953, this crossroads in my life landed squarely in the decade of the 1960s.

The school I attended beginning in the fifth grade was a small Spanish-style elementary school in the middle of the hamlet of Corona, California. It was there that my brother Ray and I had come to live with our parents, with the addition of our new baby sister, Laura, when my father took the position of chief financial officer of Corona Foothill Lemon Company, the largest Sunkist cooperative in the country at the time. I would live in this lower-middle-class, mostly Hispanic village until I went off to college.

As I write this now, it occurs to me that my basic inclination to see things in a positive light, combined with a lifetime of developing an image to match that tendency, might mislead the average reader. In moving to Utah and, later, Corona, I had permanently left behind the upper-middle-class life that I had enjoyed in San Diego. Now I was a full member of an agricultural community where almost everyone had become resigned to scratching out a subsistence living.

My grandfather always had a hundred-dollar bill in his pocket, but now my mother spent chunks of her time clipping whatever coupons she could find so we could afford even the cheapest of commodities to support our family, which eventually grew to four boys and a girl. My memories of this time include being the last kid in my class to acquire the latest-model skateboard, or a new fleece jacket, or whatever was important to a child at the time. And with only one family car, and no buses in Corona, it wasn't unusual to have to walk a mile or two on a day that was either close to freezing or 110 degrees.

Perhaps the fact that money was hard to come by in this little town motivated me all the more to find clever solutions, but that didn't dull the difficulty of coping in this new environment. It was as if I had been introduced to a life with sharp edges as a constant reminder that every moment demanded hard work and effort. It often occurred to me that I might never escape this kind of existence. And I hated it. All around me were people who could see no way out and were living their entire lives in despondency. These daily reminders became a form of bondage, and I often felt angry, frustrated, and hopeless.

Externally, I developed the fortitude to simply ignore these restraints in favor of appearing available to any bright spot that might show up the next day. I suppose this early trait (or compensation) was the beginning of my ability to reflect what is possible rather than a hard reality that is right in front of me. But make no mistake: I braved life in a tougher set of circumstances than I ever could have imagined in my earlier years. And I emerged from these experiences emotionally saddled with many of the limiting conditionings that plague this segment of society. I was and am naturally optimistic, but these days were a test that I honestly did not know if I would survive.

One fine day in November 1963, I arrived at school a few minutes early, as I normally did, to play in the yard before classes began. Who should appear but the principal, who rarely if ever came out there. We immediately sensed that something was afoot, because he gathered all of the younger children into a group instead of the normal drill of having us fall into line by grade. He told us that something very tragic had happened, and that he would like to take us into our classroom and tell us about it.

For me, it was a march of apprehension across that dusty playground and into our classroom. As we entered, I saw that all of the adults present, as well as every one of the children, were in tears. They stood pressed together in a huddle at the front of the room to be as close as possible to a TV that someone had brought to the school that day. And then I heard a voice come over the air, announcing in grave tones that the president of the United States, John F. Kennedy, had been shot.

There was no natural place for me, at the age of ten, to fit into my intellect the concept of the assassination of the leader of my culture. And if there was no room for the idea of a cataclysmic assassination, there certainly was no place in the body of that small child to take in the roomful of grief that all of us, adults included, were invited to share. I could register the pouring out of that grief, but what was I to do with it? Not only did I feel overwhelmed, I felt confused. How was I to act in this moment? And for this child, not knowing how to act was the biggest danger, for it was at those times that bad things happened in my life.

In what felt like way too short a time after JFK's murder, Martin Luther King, Jr., was assassinated in April 1968 and then, only months later, the president's brother Robert F. Kennedy. Beloved icons that represented the essence of life to a young teenager in that musical era would also leave in a hurried fashion: Jimi Hendrix, Janis Joplin, Jim Morrison, and several others would all make exits that created indelible impressions on my fast-developing sixties persona.

I had learned by the time these later deaths occurred how to behave in such situations, but I never could evade the squall of emotions—my own embroiled with everyone else's—that no container seemed capable of holding. It was in this environment that the question of where intellect leaves off and experience starts became especially acute.

It was about this time that I first read the story of Siddhartha by Hermann Hesse, and I felt as though I, too, had discovered death. It's not that I was faced with the same circumstances as the young man who would later be known as the Buddha. Throughout his youth, his parents had deliberately shielded him from seeing or even knowing about illness, old age, or death; I, on the other hand, had seen plenty of all those things. Siddhartha's experiences were different, but I felt connected to him through an energetic resonance with the same disturbing sense that something was seriously wrong here. As Hesse's book revealed to me, Siddhartha found the way through. But that discomforting feeling continued to plague me, and all I knew how to do was go outside of myself to develop a coping strategy. Only much later in life did I realize that the key that had been hidden inside of the Buddha all along was also available to me.

During this period, my family was still on its meteoric rise in the Mormon Church. I often call the immersion in Mormonism a cultural experience—that is to say, an experience that involves much more than religion. Why? Because you are never for one moment left to forget that this is the only group to which you will ever belong. Being part of the Mormon fold is always presented as the only bona fide membership for a human being. Despite its aggressive and off-putting need to be the only truth, however, many things in the Mormon religion attracted a young man such as myself. Mormonism is unique in its combination of intellectual and philosophical underpinnings mixed with a solid lower-middle-class work ethic, bound together by the passion that accompanies that class of folk. There is much to be said for that.

Remember that I had moved away from the intellectual presence of a Northern California grandfather into the culture of an agricultural village with all its conservative tendencies. So I was left to reconcile these disparate influences at a time when the environment itself was in constant flux. In my own front room, I watched on our black-and-white TV the stark, existential images of buildings burning in the Watts riots in Los Angeles or banks in flames in the suburban cities of Santa Barbara and Ventura. Songs on the radio cried out against war and rebellion and the insanity of the society that would ask its young to die.

At the same time, the Flower Children were experimenting with anything and everything they hoped would spread love and peace in the world. So, having a grandfather who had always urged me to explore, belonging to a society in which skepticism of new ideas was commonly accepted, and just being a teenager, I was at the perfect age and in the right situation to engage in a thorough examination of any set of new ideas. To wit, I was ideally situated to take on the Mormon challenge.

Despite the era's willingness to critique and reject unexamined approaches, as well as my own leanings in that direction, I still remained available to the call of authenticity and its expression. That, it seemed to me, was part of my birthright. So, yes, I saw Mormonism as a restrictive and intrusive institution laden with too many blind minions ready to sing the company song, but real passion could always find a home with me. Whenever I came across someone who, through their passion, had found truth, I responded as a brother in arms.

I will never forget the first time I happened upon a book titled *The Autobiography of Parley P. Pratt*. Here was a man who had met Joseph Smith, the founder of the Mormon religion, and was so taken by both that meeting and his subsequent reading of the translated Book of Mormon that he dedicated his whole life to the development of Mormonism. The tale is told that the first time Pratt acquired a copy of that book, he read it all the way through in one sitting, without eating or sleeping for several days. I can completely relate to that approach. I remember many occasions when I was so enthralled by something new I wanted to learn about that I would throw myself into it in much the same manner as Mr. Pratt.

In the midst of this volatile mix served up by the sixties, and in spite of the stubborn flavor of its conservatism, Corona kept delivering opportunities that fanned the flames of the passionate seeking that was developing within me. These opportunities were almost always of the kind that allowed me to make money. Making money represented a concrete outcome that fit with the type of seeking I had engaged in at an early age. I can remember figuring out that if one took a pellet gun and shot free-growing mistletoe off the old oak trees that grew near the river that ran behind our house, the plants could easily be bagged up and sold door to door. This approach worked especially well if you donned your Boy Scout uniform. One caveat to this approach, however, is to make sure that your mother never sees you do such a thing. That is, if she's on the board of directors of your local Scout chapter. Mom found no humor—or honor—in my appropriating the image of the honest, upstanding Boy Scout to inspire people to dig into their pockets for my personal gain.

My life became one of learning the concepts that were constantly being delivered by my religion and society and attempting to square those with my own, on-the-ground experience. For example, I was able to feel myself present in the here and now, so when someone would explain to me that there is a God somewhere—that is, someplace different from where I was—this didn't compute. I was beginning to get a clearer sense of what I had intuited in childhood: that whenever something that cannot be directly encountered or understood through experience is grasped by the mind and reduced to a concept, almost everyone around me immediately becomes more comfortable.

And so it appeared to me that to talk about a God that is unseen and unfelt is to talk about a God that is useless in real experience. In the conceptual realm, everything is available to be reordered and reassembled at a distance, but any God who would be real in my eyes needed to be capable of containing the overflow of uncontainable emotional experiences that overran this boy's boundaries.

This brings to mind the vivid memory of the first time that I experienced sex. This was one of the most wonderful moments I can ever remember. As you can imagine, the Mormon Church taught me that sex in any situation other than marriage was not a good thing. But I can tell you that a fifteen-and-a-half-year-old boy with the ability to enjoy his body could not find one thing wrong with the pleasure he felt. In fact, that experience fostered in me a lifelong distrust for the pronouncements of pundits, especially their opinions about experience.

As for the young teenage warrior with a predilection for passion, he was left with the jagged, unresolved pieces of all the things in his experience that didn't fit together. Internally, he began to learn how to contain these contradictions, all the while polishing external appearances so that people would think all was well. But the storms of conflict raged close to the surface as he tried hard to fill the space of uncertainty with admirable achievements and accomplishments.

How could someone so successful at so much be in continual internal upheaval? That question has been asked of me many times. The only answer I can give is that the sprouts of a future seeker were making their way to the top in the soil of his still-young soul.

5   Dancing with Mormons

As I was finishing up my years in Corona and looking ahead to a much-anticipated entry into college, it wasn't apparent whether I was more a dedicated follower of the Mormon religion or a stalwart participant in the sex, drugs, and rock 'n' roll environment of the sixties. One thing was indisputable—I was a dedicated worker. At fourteen, I started doing the lowliest, most menial jobs in the Sunkist packinghouse in Corona, happy to be one of the few kids in town who had a job.

The temperature was hovering around a hundred degrees when I showed up for my first day, which was normal for that time of year. I was handed two kneepads, a bag of oily sawdust, and the bristle end of a long broom, and summarily sent to crawl under a large conglomeration of equipment called a sizer. There were five of them in our small packinghouse, and each covered an area approximately a quarter of the size of a football field. Their purpose was to sort the various citrus fruits into appropriate bins for the packing process that would take place later. Large numbers of assorted critters found their final resting place on the floor underneath. My job was to spread the oil-soaked sawdust and sweep up deceased fruit flies, other bugs, small rodents, dead oranges, and anything else that had accumulated on the fifty-year-old waxed floors. It took about two hours on my hands and knees to clean underneath one sizer. This task stills stands as my qualifier of whether a person has done "real work" in their life—if you'd made it through anything approaching that kind of effort, you were in the club. I gladly did this job one Saturday every month for the next four years, until I finished high school.

During this time, I also attended various functions of the Mormon Church, including an hour of seminary instruction every morning prior to my first class. This was held in a church classroom conveniently located across the street from the school. The instruction period started at six-thirty sharp (Mormons always begin on time), so getting up at five-thirty to attack a day was an early discipline. At any given time, I was involved in multiple activities at school, for there didn't seem to be much in the way of experience that I did not want to try. I was fairly accomplished at several sports, earning letters in football, basketball, and baseball. I was elected class president and also learned to play the clarinet and saxophone in the school band. In addition to the normal school activities, the endless variety of possibilities that could be sampled in the sixties and seventies were not wasted on me–I did it all. Whether it was the sense of no limits that my grandfather gifted to me, or my mother's loving embrace of the same, or just good old-fashioned DNA, I was always game.

In order to take advantage of all of these opportunities, I felt compelled to develop the chameleon-like ability to live life in divergent, often diametrically opposed, environments while making sure that the stories and events worked for all who subscribed to them. It's not that I didn't enjoy all the things I was doing, or that I got no satisfaction from my achievements, but beneath the Golden Boy surface lurked an ever-present churning that became my constant companion. Simply put, there seemed to be no way to make all of Alan fit into any one set of values, dreams, or perceptions about how life should be lived. This would be the main theme of my life continuing through my early treks to India.

When I was able to graduate a year early from high school, I did so enthusiastically and used the time to attend a local junior college. I ended up dropping all of my classes for both semesters, in favor of spending most of my time in the student lounge smoking dope and learning how to play poker. A year later, when BYU came calling, I got accepted as though I were the perfect Mormon child. The admissions board had no record of my "lost year," so I could slide in without their ever knowing about it. These kinds of secrets became commonplace in my strategic approach to living in a fragmented world that seemed to require a different extraction of data and the corresponding behavior for each setting. Intuitively, I began to understand that one's stance in life is simply made up. Everything would hold together as long as one could convincingly play out a fiction that, with some effort, could be properly managed to satisfy everyone.

Another major theme of this era was the continuing conflict between what I was being taught and what I could see with my own eyes. However, it was not by a long shot that the "book learning" I was exposed to in those years could be called useless. I'd always had a predilection for learning, encouraged by my grandfather, who had given me a set of *Great Books of the Western World* when I was twelve. First released in 1952 by Encyclopedia Britannica, these attempted to capture, in fifty-four volumes, the best of human thought down the ages. Selections from the original works of Homer, Plato, Aristotle, Ptolemy, Kepler, Aquinas, Shakespeare, Cervantes, Descartes, Milton, Newton, Smith, Gibbon, Hegel, Freud, Goethe, and Darwin were all there, to name a few. Not knowing that these books were meant to be reference material, I read the entire set from cover to cover. I had no idea that people didn't do that. And it never occurred to me that it couldn't be done.

Meanwhile, I was receiving ongoing instruction on how to obey the commandments of God in my own religion, so, in my usual manner, I undertook the consumption of all the scriptures and major written works that constituted Mormon theology. With all of that as a background, it was easy for me to continue absorbing knowledge throughout my school years. As was common in that era, my formal education emphasized absorbing information and regurgitating the important pieces so that some teacher would give me a grade that would place me within the correct stratum of society. I was good at that, but I always felt shortchanged. I knew how much more my mind could do, and how much more robust my education would be, if it included real experience. In addition, when one lives in an agricultural village and is witness to the love that men show for the trees and fruit they nurture daily, it becomes evident that book learning, by itself, is only a distant reflection of reality.

Unable to find a place where all the parts of Alan could fit together, I had to settle for finding a way to operate in separate spheres as my culture had created them. I always hid my good grades because the people I was hanging out with at the time would have never understood why anyone would go to such great effort to attain them. If I had been found out, I wouldn't have been one of the guys. I saw this as a necessary part of my strategy for managing the multiple environments in which I lived.

In the midst of this manipulation, however, the felt reality of passion would make itself known. The people I loved most were those who came from the earth. They worked hard, spoke simply, and encouraged me to reach for the heights. The packinghouse in Corona was manned mostly by Mexican Americans, most of whom spoke little or no English. It was these folks who arrived each day with a homemade burrito for the young gringo, along with admonitions that I reach for the kinds of opportunities they knew they would never have.

Some years later, when I saw the famous scene in the movie *An Officer and a Gentleman* in which the hero returns to the textile factory to sweep his girl off her feet and carry her away, I knew that feeling. In every instance, these friends who had taught me how to work, and had been my beloved cheerleaders from the very beginning, would always celebrate the fact that I had taken advantage of the opportunities that had been so richly bestowed on me. Until the day it closed, I went back to that packinghouse many times during my college and career days.

I was accepted to begin study at Brigham Young University in the fall of 1971, at the age of eighteen. With the hope of becoming a professor of philosophy, I enrolled myself in a graduate seminar in the Philosophy Department during the second semester of my first year. This was a typical "Alan move," as it would later be called by my wives and children. In the days before computers that could flag impostors like myself, who would know that I was only a freshman? I could simply show up and prove that I belonged there—notwithstanding the evidence that I still hadn't started to shave. So, in the midst of this elite group of dedicated graduate students, I plunged undetected into an area of study called religious symbology, which covers the emergence of meaning from the ineffable into the describable.

This class was conducted by the most revered philosophy professor at Brigham Young at the time, Truman Madsen. He held a chair at Harvard University and was recognized by the philosophy world as one of the finest thinkers of the time. I still cherish the memory of my first reading of Martin Buber for that class. Here was a man whose tender love of God leapt off the pages and into my imagination.

At first, I was not taken very seriously by my classmates. Mr. Madsen, however, seemed to enjoy the questions I asked and was always encouraging whenever we stopped to chat on campus. The grade for this class would be based entirely on a paper that was to be turned in at the end of the semester. One of the proudest moments of my student life occurred when I received the highest grade in the class. Slanted across the top of the cover page in Mr. Madsen's careful penmanship were these words:

Lucidly written, and of the highest caliber of clarity.

A-

I have given you the minus for the simple reason that you are a freshman.

I still have that paper today.

One cannot live a life of conflicting themes that are separated, packaged, and presented to one's various audiences without an understanding of the ego beginning to emerge. In all of my experience and in all I had read, I had been constantly taught that there is something called a core self. In fact, I was often told that the purpose of life is to find this core self. That assumption seemed inherent in the formulation of someone no less illustrious than Socrates himself, "Know thyself." Obviously, this admonition was predicated on the existence of an individualized ego-self that could be known. But my experience of slipping seamlessly between multiple ego-definitions according to the intuited need of the moment flew in the face of what I imagined a core self to be.

Although I could see that something that we agree to call an ego develops as a mechanism of self-protection in response to an environment that demands conformity, I wasn't sure that there was such a thing as a core self in the being called Alan. All I knew was that the multiplicity of demands for the required responses and behaviors produced in me various patterned ways that all seemed to work, given a little practice. Each of these ways I experienced as an extension of the "myself" that everyone else presumed existed—and that's as far as I could take it.

I completed my first semester of study at BYU in a somewhat dismal fashion and embarked on my second, which would not end any better. With the exception of advanced philosophy, I was obviously not distinguishing myself academically. By the end of my first year, I saw no way forward to continue this course of study. For about five years now, I had fully partaken of two distinctive styles of life, Mormon and non-Mormon. And the tumult lurking underneath my well-packaged exterior had left me in a fix. It was during this time that an interesting decision began to emerge.

On the Mormon side of life, a male who has attained nineteen years of age is expected to voluntarily commit to a two-year full-time mission as a proselytizer, generally in a foreign country. There began to arise in me a desire to serve on such a mission. Throughout my life, many people have asked me why. I suppose that the passion I saw in those who had served on a mission could have been alluring. But I was unable to identify any particular trigger for my decision. So I often told folks that I went to make my mother happy. To be entirely honest, there was no specific reason other than the emerging of the desire itself.

So, in early March of 1972, I filled out a tedious and complicated application and took a language-learning aptitude test. I thought that the best place to go would be a country where German was spoken; this,

I reasoned, would boost the possibility of a future philosophy professorship. So I wrote this request across the top of the front page of my application.

The moment arrived one Saturday morning when my mother called from Corona with the news that a large envelope had just arrived at the door. I immediately gave her permission to open it to find out where her eldest son was to spend the next two years of his life. In the usual stiff prose of Mormon communications, the letter said that I was to serve the Mormon Church in the country of Peru, leaving on June 24, 1972. Now, my mother and I were not known as the greatest of geographers; we both were sent scurrying for a map to find out where exactly we might find this Peru place. To our surprise, we found out that it is located in some of the highest mountains on Earth, called the Andes. We also discovered that it was an incredibly poor country and that the language I would learn was Spanish. I confess that my first reaction was disappointment that I wouldn't be learning German, but that was soon replaced by the excitement of anticipating new adventures.

One of the most interesting collisions during the ongoing effort to manage my two realities occurred in the process of applying for a mission. It turns out that the voluminous forms I had filled out had included questions about my personal habits and activities. As I read them, the intent arose to be completely sincere in my answers. That meant revealing particulars concerning my clandestine activities with drugs, sex, and other such pursuits common to young adults indigenous to the culture of the American sixties.

Unbeknownst to me, it was common practice for any prospective missionary who answered the application questions in the way I did to be interviewed by what is referred to in Mormon circles as a general authority. For those not familiar with Mormon theology: It is scripturally held that from the time of Jesus Christ up to the revelations of the first Mormon prophet, Joseph Smith, there was no direct communication by God to humans on Earth. With the formation of the Mormon Church, God remedied that situation by calling into service a succession of men who have held his priesthood, restoring to them the job of being prophets or prophets-in-waiting. It was by one of these men that I was to be interviewed for a period of approximately two hours. The outcome would determine whether or not I would go to Peru.

I remember clearly that day in early May when I made the drive from Provo forty-five miles north to the LDS headquarters in Salt Lake City. It was a cloudy, cold day, perfectly suited for an inquisition. I had been ordered to report to a fellow named Loren C. Dunn, a man whose six-foot, seven-inch frame was as intimidating when folded into the straight-backed chair behind his sturdy desk as when it stood towering above me. An interlocutor of this type offers no introductory small talk to create ease in the conversation. I was immediately directed to describe my nefarious deeds, which he already knew were those of anyone but a faithful Mormon youth. His voice, steely after many years of training to convey no affect at all, pressed in for the details:

ELDER DUNN: How many times did you have sex?

Now this is a question that you might ask a person who has experience in measured amounts. I can assure you that my experiments with the opposite sex occurred in such a way that no meter could have captured the torrential flow.

ALAN: Is it necessary for me to have counted how many times I have had sex?

ELDER DUNN: How many kinds of drugs have you used?

ALAN: Sir, I don't believe I have ever kept count of such a thing.

ELDER DUNN: And Brother Shelton, how many times did you use each of the kinds of drugs that you used?

I wasn't sure why he thought I could come up with an answer to that, since I hadn't been able to give him one for the other two questions. Once again, I had to confess that there would have been no way to capture a count of my activities.

To this day, I do not understand why I was approved for my mission, given the ragged experience of that interview. I did, however, learn that it would be wise to resume my strategy of distributing the right stories to the right audiences. Looking back, I recognize a pattern of attempting to present all of myself whenever I began a new stage of life. When in my natural nest of passion, I never felt required to shape or reduce the dimensions of my experience. And the urge to extend that fullness into a presentation of self that would be welcomed by others never left me. However, it was confirmed again and again that the consensus collective in the majority of those situations wanted only the pieces of Alan that fit with their own values and agendas.

And so it is in the pursuit of self-mastery: We want only the attributes that are to our liking to emerge and be seen by others. We become the sculptors of our personality, carefully carving into shape the chunks that we want to preserve and tossing out the rest. At least, that is the attempt. If that were possible, our world would appear as a perfect Mt. Rushmore, with all our meticulously formed little faces peeking out from the jaggedness of experience. The fact that no one can ever produce a flawless piece of art should give us our first clue that the self-mastery approach to shaping individuals may not work.

6 The Real Mountains of Peru

In the development of every ego, there comes a time when it is called to perform in a consistent, focused, and adult way. Yes, there had been evidence that the warrior child who sold chocolates, wrote philosophy, and toiled under mammoth machines on his hands and knees would be able to do just that. But no challenge had ever arisen that required complete, daily focus for an extended period of time. Being called to a mission in Peru was the first test of whether the passion to climb mountains of achievement that was his natural style could be sustained in an environment so demanding that lasting two months there, much less two years, seemed like an impossible task.

At the time I left for Peru, I had no idea that my journey through life would continue to configure itself in the shape of the apparently undoable. It would take years of experience in different settings before I recognized that the impossible kept showing up like calling cards that, often when least expected, beckoned me to addresses that did not appear anywhere on my internal map. But pursue them I did, propelled into vortices of the unknown that had an attraction I couldn't refuse.

It can often appear that the passionate behavior observed in people who are engaged in activities demanding single-minded focus is without conflict. In my case, nothing could be further from the truth. The constant battle to keep hidden under my pleasing exterior the pieces that didn't match that image required an exhausting vigilance. I was split between the compulsion to succeed and the fear that I would be found out.

Nevertheless, underneath that passionate, conflicted achiever lurked the seeker who would make his appearance later on. You see, in the years leading up to my mission, I had been repeatedly told that if I applied myself to the question of whether it is possible for a human being to know truth, God would not only answer me, he would also reveal that truth to me. This idea had some traction with me, thanks to my aforementioned favorite book, *The Autobiography of Parley P. Pratt*. For I had touched the passion of another human being who, in addition to taking on the challenge of a mission, had found what appeared to be his own personal truth.

It wasn't until much later that I would become a real seeker chasing after something authentic in experience. At nineteen, I still saw the enterprise known as "finding the truth" akin to building a career. It was less a natural draw to the light than a push toward another, supposedly more desirable, type of achievement. And so it was that I, enamored with establishing the definition of my performing ego and its self-mastery, was not ready to seek out the deepest truths of life that I suspected existed. On the other hand, the promise that I would find truth in real experience was more than an abstract idea; it was a call that already existed somewhere deeper in me than mere intellectual suspicion. It simply would take years of maturing before my need for ego-definition and my intellectual attempts to find truth through an exploration of philosophy were superseded by something far more real.

Years later, while listening to my guru in India, I heard a story that I eventually found out is one of Aesop's fables. It goes like this:

A scorpion and a frog meet on the bank of a stream, and the scorpion asks the frog to carry him across on its back. The frog, who is of course wary, asks, "How do I know you won't sting me?"

The scorpion answers, "Because if I do, I will die too."

The frog is satisfied, and the two set out. But midstream, the scorpion stings the frog. Feeling the onset of paralysis and starting to sink, the frog has just enough time to gasp, "Why?"

Replies the scorpion, "It is my nature . . ."

The well-meaning and well thought out request by the scorpion is ultimately trumped by the scorpion's very nature. And in the end, the scorpion himself recognizes this very fact. In the same way, it is possible, after years of intellectual development, to present oneself in a certain image, but midcrossing, the nature of the beast will win out. And so it was that no matter how polished my exterior might appear, passion always sought a fissure through which it could find its way out. And those geysers of energy did not land in my life with any of the polite precision I hoped they might.

Lest you think that I was tossed into the Peru experience with no preparation, I will tell you a bit about the training that preceded the mission itself. With no little trepidation, I reported to Salt Lake City along with five hundred other nineteen-year-old boys for a period of intense indoctrination into the rules of mission life. After five days of being drilled, the twelve of us who had been preselected to go to the Peruvian section of the language-training mission in Provo were sent on our way.

Language training for Mormon missionaries is based on the same system used for teaching specialists in the U.S. armed services. It was not uncommon for the Defense Language Institute in Monterey, California, which taught military operatives, to exchange teachers with those assigned to Mormon LTM. Each day included eight hours of classroom instruction followed by four hours of intensive homework. A normal day would begin at five-thirty in the morning and end at ten at night, with every activity taking place in the confines of the same building. With the exception of a half-day per week, the entire time was dedicated to learning Spanish. This meant that from the moment one arrived, English was virtually off limits. You were armed with a dictionary and told that for the next two months you could speak your native language only during that half-day "off," which was mostly swallowed up by doing laundry and other errands.

Those months held few, if any, anecdotes interesting enough to report, so I have no snappy nuggets to offer. Indelible in my memory, however, is the music that I listened to whenever I could, for it was the only audible feature outside of Spanish immersion that was allowed to filter into my world. Neil Young and Cat Stevens were two of my closest friends during that time. I can tell you that it is those guys who got me through an endurance test that was much harder than it needed to be. The classrooms we were forced to sit in were intolerably hot and, on top of that, I had contracted mononucleosis during my few days in Salt Lake City, so I started most of my days in Provo already exhausted.

My response to these circumstances was to take the same leap into action as when my father pointed out how I could get that red hatchet: I set about to unleash my all. The challenges of Mormon boot camp reactivated that inner drive to win, which refused to be vanquished. No particular truth about life was revealed to me during that time, and the various parts that made up an "Alan" were as uncontainable as ever. But I can honestly say that at the end of those weeks of unceasing effort, I was convinced that I could conquer just about anything and declare, much as the scorpion did, "It is my nature."

So it was with an air of heightened confidence that, in August 1974, I boarded the plane that was to take me to Peru for the next twenty-two months. Not only had I just survived the most difficult two months of my life, I also felt that I had developed a good feel for the Spanish language and would easily be able to navigate the next chapter of this adventure.

I soon found out that the reality was much different than I had pictured, and that it was intent on crashing into my life on its own terms.

In those days, it was against Peruvian law to possess American dollars. Upon arrival at the airport, one would be ushered to a cashier's window where dollars got surrendered for multicolored pieces of paper that looked more suitable for a game of Monopoly. Now, you may think that the human ego does not pay attention to the familiar objects that it encounters in daily life. But I can tell you that, at my age, the habit of using dollars as a currency was an indelible one.

My memory of this event is of a very frustrated Peruvian woman frowning from behind the glass, speaking to me too quickly in a language that hardly seemed like any of the Spanish I had learned. Further, she was demanding that I hand over to her the only thing that was still familiar to me—my money. So I left the Lima airport with the realization that after all I had gone through, I couldn't make myself understood when I spoke and that I was now in possession of money I had no idea how to use.

I spent my first two months in Lima learning how to navigate both the language and everyday life. I proved to be adept at adjusting to Spanish as it was spoken there, but my neat little American version of more or less civilized life was soon ripped apart. It wasn't but a few days after my arrival that the front-page headlines of the local paper blazed out the news that eleven members and coaches of the Israeli athletic team had been taken hostage and killed at the Olympics in Munich. I struggled to account for how the big, unruly world behaved. Back at home, I had, in my own American way, learned how to feel secure in the face of these sorts of events. But here, there was no United States of America to keep me safe.

Closer to my daily reality, I also learned that one of the young missionaries I'd recently met had just jumped to his death off the cliffs of Chimbote, 250 miles north of Lima. Apparently, he didn't think he could make it through the two years and, being from a noted Mormon family, could not face the prospect of returning to Utah in disgrace. I could not comprehend how death could possibly be a better outcome than disgrace. When the initial thunderclap of shock faded, I was left with a sore heart. This feeling was still new, but it was starting to enter into my world far too often.

After Lima, I was sent to Chiclayo, a beautiful city on the coast of northern Peru with weather much like that of my beloved California. I inherited as my companion a homespun kid from the weeds of Wyoming, Bruce Morrison, who had already been in the city for a couple of months. All missionaries are assigned a companion and, when on a mission, the two of you are always—and that means always—required to be together. And you are to address one another only by the title "Elder," followed by the last name. In contrast to these and other stringent rules, missionaries are given wide latitude in their choice of where to spend their time. So it came as a big surprise that in my first days there, Elder Morrison said that we would be visiting a ghetto area some distance away rather than a more upscale neighborhood close by.

The homes in this village were made of thatched reeds, the floors were dirt, and the sewers ran openly in ditches in the middle of the dusty roads. Here we met four or five families, all of which had small children who moved like nimble deer in the crowded roads. A love as tender as it was unexpected immediately sprang up between us and these children, and it didn't take much time for Elder Morrison and me to figure out that they would be the key to improving our Spanish as well. These little ones had no adult embarrassment about correcting any of the words and sentences that they found unacceptable to their ear. You can imagine how much at home the two elders, who were really just a pair of farm boys, felt with these poorest of Peruvian peasant children. They became our fast friends.

In these early days, the dirt and poverty felt oppressive and, given that the pueblo was in a desert climate, it came as no surprise when a heat wave would arise to make living conditions all the more stifling. One morning, Elder Morrison and I woke up and noticed the kind of clear sky and early heat that, in the Mojave Desert, means you are in for a very hot, very long day. It was quite a hike to the village, so we chose to spend that day much nearer to the coast and to wait a day or two until the temperature dropped before we returned. All normal work in the area had come to a halt. The noisy bustle of trucks ceased, leaving the city streets strangely silent. We were two heat-sapped zombies, struggling to simply make it through each day. Two days stretched to three, and then four. By then, accounts were appearing in the newspaper that the heat wave had caused havoc in some of the smaller, more out-of-the-way villages.

When it was cool enough to return to the pueblo, we set out in the early morning and made our way there. We found not a single person on the street. Finally, we knocked on the door of one of our houses. A man with a small frame bent from a life of pain and hardship, but whom I knew as an unwavering source of good cheer, appeared at the door with a tear-stained face. In a voice that can come only from a father who has felt devastating loss, he somehow formed the words that both of his children were dead. Not only that—two more of our children, who lived a couple of doors down, had also died. The truck that provided the sole supply of water for the town, which we had noticed on some of our earlier visits, had run out of water before it got to the pueblo at the top of the hill.

My heart was changed forever. These kids were mine in a way that only an awkward nineteen-year-old who is just learning to love understands. And now they were gone. Nothing I had ever experienced had prepared me for the finality of these deaths. Once again, I had nowhere to put everything that was making itself felt in that moment. The pain went even deeper than the sense of personal loss. I had been sent to make a difference in the lives of those I was serving, and when it came to the difference that counted most, I had been powerless. The frustration that wrapped itself around my sorrow overshadowed my passion for the entire missionary system. I went for days and nights unable to sleep, for the death of those children challenged the very assumptions that all achievers and performers take as their basis for living and cherish as their birthright. I did not want to accept that, in any moment, what matters most to us can be swept away in the unpredictability of forces that lie beyond our attempts to control life through our plans, our rules, and even our dedication to the highest principles.

At this point, it was only an inkling, but the notion that we are the authors of our own activity was coming into question and starting to lose its stability in my world. Still, like most of us do, I continued to drive toward a perfect self, believing that such a thing is possible. I simply ignored any elements of my experience that contravened the need to remain in control of my life, so that they wouldn't get in my way. Years later, I would scoop these up as valuable pointers to another possibility.

Four months passed, and I was transferred back to Lima and spent a lot of my time in another ghetto plagued with poverty, open sewers, stray dogs, and beautiful people who worked hard to change their circumstances.

The one constant I could rely on was the discipline I had created to accomplish the tasks that a mission demanded. Our schedule was divided into two kinds of work. We were expected to proselytize—to knock on doors and engage in spiritual discussions—for seventy hours weekly. Required study of religious and scriptural texts filled an additional thirty hours a week. We tumbled out of bed every morning, without fail, at five-thirty and turned in at ten-thirty every night. And there was that one half-day that was left to do errands, wash our clothes, and attempt any outings. Later, when I was at Lake Titicaca, twice a week I'd walk the four or five blocks to a hotel where I could pay ten or eleven *soles*—about twenty-five cents—and have a hot shower down in the basement. The rest of the time, we had to boil water on a sterno stove for washing and shaving. For the entire two years of my mission, I took it upon myself to never waver from this schedule.

Within this framework of strict discipline, my drive to find the truth spurred me on to pour out more and more effort. I used my weekly study hours to read the Bible, the Book of Mormon, Doctrine and Covenants, and myriad theological treatises many times over. I became comfortable with the most obtuse of theological writing, even to the point of enjoyment.

All that hard work and discipline did not go unnoticed. For the remainder of my mission, I was chosen to fill a series of the highest leadership posts. After the first year, I became a zone leader, which meant being in charge of 140 missionaries throughout the entire southern region of Peru. I was based in Arequipa, the second largest city in the country.

Just as I was arriving there, the then president of Chile, Salvador Allende, was killed in a coup, and a brutal military dictatorship took his place. My experience of these events was of witnessing the refugees who poured over the border into our city and, in some cases, interacting with them. I had never spoken to anyone whose family members had been rounded up, forced into a sports stadium, and summarily executed. It was common knowledge in that part of the world that the United States government had been the principal architect of a massacre in which thousands of individuals had been murdered. Admitting to myself that this was true permanently changed the view I had of my own country. Had I not been there during this event, I am sure I would have never believed that my own countrymen were capable of such a deed. Yet here it was in front of my face.

Later that year, I would see the brutality of the Peruvian government against its own citizens. At one point, the government doubled the price of cooking oil. This ignited the indignation of the Peruvian women and seemed to be the deciding factor that drove the city of Arequipa to attempt secession. (Imagine Chicago notifying the feds that it no longer considers itself part of the United States, and then proceeding to conduct its affairs as though that were the case.) As is common in this kind of civil unrest, students from the various universities in the city were major participants. As luck would have it, I lived across the street from the medical university. On about the third day of rioting in the streets, I received a call from Lima, informing me that the army had been sent in full force to invade the city. I immediately phoned all of my missionaries to order them to stay in their homes. Two of my newbies, probably eager for some adventure and assuming that they were capable of independent judgment, were nowhere to be found, so I felt that I had no choice except to venture out into the city to find them.

I was scarcely two blocks from the house of the Mormon family where I was staying when I felt a large brick careen off the right side of my head. This left my companion for this segment of my mission, Elder Hoyt, to drag me back to the house. My encounter with the brick turned out to be fortuitous, for the tanks entered the city twenty minutes later. I watched through our window as students were slaughtered in the streets, with dump trucks following the action to collect the bodies and transport them to a place where they would never be seen again. To this day, there are families in Peru that do not know where or how their sons and daughters attending the universities met their end on that day. Nor have the bodies ever been found.

As for our missing missionaries, they had returned to the home where they were lodged as soon as they saw helicopters firing over our section of town. The safety of our whole contingent was somewhat inaccurately credited to me as their leader and, soon afterward, I was called to be a branch president of a congregation in a mountain town of some thirty thousand souls. A branch president in Mormon terms is roughly the same as a pastor or a bishop, depending on what denominations we're talking about. So, in this town called Puno, on the shores of Lake Titicaca, I was thrust into yet another new environment, having inherited a congregation of about two hundred people and the responsibility for the religious life of not only families and missionaries but also possible converts.

It was during this time that I was called on to excommunicate a member of the Church for blasphemous writings. Discharging this responsibility was both awkward and difficult, for I didn't believe that his writing was an injury to the Church or anyone else. The entire affair was weighed down by the heavy energy of accusation and judgment that the three others on the tribunal felt toward this fellow. On the other end of the spectrum were experiences such as performing a joyous marriage ceremony for a nervous but innocent young couple. As my duties—pleasant or not—and the skills needed to exercise them expanded, I expanded with them. Indeed, a young man of twenty had been placed in a leadership role that would advise his approach to the rest of his life.

By the time I arrived at the end of my mission experience, I had fulfilled all of my responsibilities in a way that pleased my superiors, plus I now spoke fluent, perfectly accented Spanish. Most important to me, however, I had found my heart in this country of harrowing contrasts. I had not, however, received any spiritual confirmation regarding the Mormon belief system. My experiences in Peru created in me a formidable capacity to manage people and circumstances that would serve me well in the future. I was left only with the challenges themselves and no reliable spiritual lens through which to view them. I felt bitter that—unlike the experience of my hero, Pratt—my inner thirst for truth and all of my efforts to discover it hadn't produced anything that I could revel in. I was deeply disappointed that Mormonism wasn't likely to ever deliver on its promise of truth.

I had been taught well enough that it is a noble thing to strive for goals defined by others as being worthy. In the absence of anything of a religious or spiritual nature that satisfied my mind or my heart, I would soon set myself toward honorably working my way down a prescribed list of worldly accomplishments, half hoping that I would somehow find along the way the deeper truths that I sought. Armed now with new capacities and a confidence born of experience that made almost anything seem achievable, I became determined to tick one thing after another off that list.

7   Driving Self-Mastery

Some years ago, a fellow seeker and corporate CEO who is a dear friend of mine, Jerry Skillett, shared a story that I often tell to both leadership aspirants and spiritual seekers.

A cook of some renown came to discover that he was very good at making delicious coconut pies. He assembled a competent staff of pastry chefs and, in short order, became the leading coconut pie maker in the country. With such success, it soon came time to call in the business consultants for their wisdom. Their main suggestion was to expand the product line and begin making banana pies. The cook decided that the best approach was to duplicate every activity that had made him successful in the coconut pie business. He insisted that his purchasers buy the best ingredients; he employed better and even more fastidious assistants; and with the exception of a new label, he used the same packaging that had attracted so many buyers.

So it came as a surprise when the consultants, who eagerly returned to taste the new product, could only look at the cook in confusion. The pie was as delicious as ever, they told him, but they could not tell the difference between the banana pie that was in front of them and the coconut pie they had grown to love.

In reexamining their process, the cook and his staff discovered that while they had copied every single activity perfectly, they had neglected to add a new ingredient called bananas.

Often in the life of an individual, a sense arises that one is in a place to make a decision that will lead in a new direction. But once this decision is made, it is just as often discovered that the choice has initiated a journey of endless duplication. It wasn't exactly this place that I found myself upon returning from the country of Peru, but I was definitely in the neighborhood. I still felt the pull toward an exploration of inner experience, but I also had just completed the first leg of an incredibly successful outer journey of achievement in production. It was probably inevitable that the next stage of my life would consist primarily of developing what I call the ego-performer, in the most polished and crystallized form possible. I would not have turned my back on any of the deeper truths of life had they arrived on my doorstep, but the fruits of an achievement-oriented career were low-hanging and ready to be picked. So I threw myself even more enthusiastically into the process of self-mastery, with ample help from those around me.

One of the first things that happened upon my return to BYU was a conversation initiated by the chairman of the Philosophy Department. It was still my intention to complete a degree in philosophy—focused on mythological and religious content but with an intellectual approach—with an eye to a career of teaching this subject that I loved so much. But even philosophers can be practical, and this kind man felt duty-bound to advise me that there would most likely be no jobs for philosophy teachers in the next several decades. If I wanted to be self-supportive, he said, I should find something of practical value that I could do in the real world.

For a young man born in the flowerbed of business acumen and financial theory, this was fairly easy advice to take. (I have often said that if you want to survive a Thanksgiving dinner with my family, you should be able to discuss economic theory at length.) So I began to take classes in accounting as well as philosophy. It was during this time that I began to be exposed to the concepts of leadership that were emerging in that era. I was fortunate to be a student of a then little-known professor, Stephen Covey. And later I would study with another professor, Terry Warner, whose philosophy would spawn the classic work entitled

Leadership and Self-Deception. Some of the seeds that would later blossom and send nourishment into my life were being planted.

As you may recall, in the year leading up to my mission, I had managed to cobble together two unimpressive academic semesters, with the exception of the graduate philosophy seminar. This miserable effort had landed me on the academic probation list, but now I launched off on a succession of five semesters on the dean's list and emerged from my academic career with a degree in two subjects, accounting and philosophy, with a minor in Spanish literature.

But the world of Alan's achievements never stayed restricted to one domain for very long. The Boy Scout who could identify a business opportunity in the form of mistletoe in the nearby dry wash had grown up into a man who apparently could apply the same ingenuity in the adult world.

When I was seventeen and eighteen, I had worked in motor-home factories in Southern California, learning both electrical and plumbing, so it was an easy stretch to become proficient enough in plumbing to land some work. Thus, my first job after returning to BYU was as a plumber assigned to student housing owned by the university. Without much effort, I was able to discern that the construction trades in Provo—specifically, plumbing—did not provide repair services. I noticed that most of the apartment complexes and multitenant properties in the area were always in need of a plumber. At the time, I was earning two-fifty an hour, but the repair rates throughout the city were hovering around the twenty-dollar mark. It didn't take a PhD to see that this could be leveraged.

So I bought a van, acquired some tools, and set out to place under contract as many units as I could handle by myself. In the first two weeks, I was able to locate enough units to keep myself occupied part-time as well as provide twenty hours of work per week for four employees. In my first year of business, I made a net profit of $30,000. This may not sound like a lot in today's terms. But when you consider that it was 1975, and that I took my first corporate job two years later at an annual salary of $13,200, it was a feat.

During that period of bustling enterprise, I was still a practicing Mormon. This meant not only faithfully attending church services, but also participating—according to one's status in the Church—in certain solemn rituals that could only be conducted in a Mormon Temple. Most of these were based loosely on Masonic rituals, which were then applied to the doctrine that had been revealed through Joseph Smith. Some of the rituals, such as those similar to the teachings in the Tibetan Book of the Dead, were based on esoteric knowledge critical for moving through the after-death process. So, as required, I had undergone the Temple rituals that ensure the passage of each foresworn individual into the Kingdom of God after death. I had a working knowledge of Mormon ceremony and, despite my doubts that I was a "true Mormon," I always had genuine respect for these rites. I thought they might one day be the doorway to the authentic experience of truth that I still longed for.

One compulsory practice, for both men and women, is the wearing of a type of long underwear referred to as garments. Sewn onto these garments are symbols that reflect the oaths taken in the Temple ceremonies. One day, as I was walking across the campus, I was stopped by a fellow I knew who was the president of my group of elders; that is, he held the priesthood at a certain level within my congregation. Unable to see the outlines under my clothes that served as evidence that I was wearing these garments, he proceeded to issue a stern lecture while I stood in the middle of the campus with students passing by, curious to know what kind of dressing-down I was getting.

The elder never asked, nor did he give me any opportunity to explain, the reason. It so happened that whenever my lifetime affliction of eczema flared up, wearing those garments was unbearable. Regardless of the particulars, my respect for what I considered to be the most personal and sacred symbols of Mormonism—not to mention my sincere quest for truth within this system—did not brook such an intrusion. Whatever remained of my waning interest in Mormonism dissolved then and there. That was the moment I ceased to be a Mormon, though I wasn't formally excommunicated until 1988.

This had the effect of freeing up time to dedicate to my career, and the next period of my life became a stroll through the park in terms of the successes that would seek me out. I graduated from BYU, having already selected from many offers the opportunity to work for Price Waterhouse, one of the largest international accounting firms. In a short three years, I passed the CPA exam and acquired the requisite skills for a CPA certificate.

It seemed that everything was conspiring to give me the kind of experience and curriculum vitae that guarantees stellar success in the corporate world. My largest client was IBM, where I was assigned to Milton Friedman, later a Nobel Prize winner in Economics, on an antitrust case. I also worked on acquisition projects for both IBM and Sunkist, using my Spanish skills in meetings and for reviewing documents. Working with luminaries such as Friedman, having high-profile clients, and quickly showing up on the map as a Spanish-speaking merger/acquisition specialist established my bona fides and advanced my career by many years.

It was not long before I spotted a gap once again in the Southern California market. While working with companies that were preparing to be acquired, I noticed that the professionals who represented them came from smaller, less experienced firms. Of course, it occurred to the mind of a twenty-six-year-old with endless confidence that he might be the one to take advantage of this insight. So, with not many years of experience under my belt, I started my own CPA firm, aimed at early-stage companies that needed help polishing their image in order to attract the highest acquisition price.

Only a few years later, I was contacted by a group of thirteen CEOs who banded together at daylong monthly meetings in my local area to process their personal and corporate issues, using their fellow CEOs as a sounding board. They invited me to join their group, which was one of many such groups in the country that had been organized by a company called The Executive Committee (TEC). Each was facilitated by a professional business coach whose full-time focus was to coordinate his group and oversee the vetting of potential members.

One day not too long into my acceptance process, the facilitator called to express his concern: My company was small and my career experience limited; what did I have that I could offer such a group?

You need to know here that the average age of these CEOs was forty-eight, and that their companies averaged one hundred employees and did between ten million and two hundred million in revenue annually. I was twenty-nine, had ten employees, and had yet to reach a million in revenue. From this position of comparative strength, I found myself responding, without missing a beat, "I am not at all concerned with what I can bring to the table; I am concerned about whether these other CEOs have the experience, insight, and intelligence to do anything for me."

Much later, he told me that, more than anything else known about me at the time, the obvious confidence underlying my response had convinced him that I "belonged in the room." He had applied the measuring stick used by most seasoned executives when intuitively sizing up a colleague, and this combination of credible brashness and ease, which was becoming second nature to me, had proved worthy of a membership invitation.

So that is how I became the cub CEO, incessantly batted about and shaped by these leaders whom I soon came to love and respect. Two years down the track, my firm, which had grown to almost a hundred employees, was exceeding ten million in revenues. By the time I was thirty-five, it was obvious to anyone who was paying attention that I had taken a dominant position in the corporate world of Southern California. I was plugged into companies such as Allergan and Pacific Mutual and was associating daily with the most well known corporate CEOs in Orange County. I also became a speaker at other CEO groups, often using the process techniques that I had learned in my own group to help management teams reach their goals. It seemed to me that there was nothing I couldn't attain in corporate terms. And since I could consistently produce in that world, I continued—reminiscent of our cook who kept on making coconut pies—to master those skills.

Some of the beliefs I had acquired since my return from Peru—political and otherwise—were consistent with the role that I filled as a businessman, and were far from the views I held in the sixties. Thus it might have appeared that I had forgotten about the tragic conditions of the poor and disadvantaged whom I had embraced in Peru. I never pushed aside what I had experienced there, but I was now functioning in a context that wasn't remotely like the setting in which those kids had died.

I don't say this to excuse my lack of attention to the harsh realities that had given birth to my love for the underdog. I simply rose to the more narrow challenge of the moment with the single-mindedness required to engage with what Existence brought to me at that time. Guilt never played a part in this, as it was always apparent to me that I couldn't help anyone without first reaching a position in life that would enable me to do that.

Nonetheless, the glimmerings of a future inner journey began to appear. Many books were being written about the transformational stages of men's growth and the challenges that males faced in the culture of that time. Two of my favorites, and also among the best known, were *Iron John* by Robert Bly and *Fire in the Belly* by Sam Keen. This "men's work" led more than a few males to drumming circles and sweat lodges, but I was never drawn to participate in these types of activities. I had readily available to me the opportunity to grow into grace by simply being in the presence of businessmen and leaders of uncompromising nature who knew how to stand in their own strength. Much like my mother and grandmother, they taught me that anytime something came at me, all I had to do was measure the rising tide and pick the appropriate moment to allow my strength to show itself. Sure enough, this approach would always win out over the Pavlovian attack-style of doing business that most young executives seem to favor.

I often reflect on the fact that the role of father figure in my life has not been filled by any one person. Life has sent me many fathers. In each successive stage of my growth, these father-men have appeared to both model their holding of the male birthright and usher me into the fullest expression of it that I could expand into at the time. It began with my grandfather, who held a little boy's hand and sat him on the kingly seat of a wise man's knee. And it continued with that group of CEOs, who seasoned me—corporate style—grinding off the rough edges of the gem that they sensed lay beneath my developing exterior. I have a special affection for these thirteen men, who took the time and care to take me under their wings and share with me whatever they knew, whenever I asked. For this I will be forever grateful. With my last grandfather, Osho, the male birthright exploded into a space with no limits—but that is a story for later.

In the meantime, I was busy building, brick by brick, a life that comprised all the elements that I had been taught would lead to fulfillment and nourishment. I got married, had two children, and bought a big house on a hillside in Orange County with a spectacular view of the ocean. I had an unlimited expense account and played golf at one of the most prestigious country clubs in the area. Many people who arrive at this point, recognizing that they have made a notable achievement, choose to live the rest of their lives in the same pattern. They hold unflinchingly to the belief that, having completed what they started out to do, there is nothing left except to enjoy the benefits that accompany that level of accomplishment.

That was not to be the case for Alan, for the niggling force of innate intelligence kept interrupting his successes to inform him that he was neither fulfilled nor nourished.

The moment eventually arrived when I recognized that I had reached the pinnacle of a corporate career—and at a much earlier time than I had expected. Within this realization, I was somehow given the grace to understand that if I was unhappy and felt empty as a human being, more of the same was not going to fix the problem. It became apparent to me that my relationships with my family, and with more than a few of the people I was encountering in my profession, had the turbulent character of most of those I observed around me.

The dissatisfaction I was feeling across the board seemed to be operating at a much deeper level than any solution my current reality could offer. No amount of leadership training, no new and exciting approach to corporate problem-solving, could deliver me out of the angst that was becoming the central theme of my existence. I might have been able to manage these feelings if they had politely stayed in the background. But whenever I let down my guard, it felt as though my insides were being pelted by hailstones that tore at my gut, leaving me battered inside where no one could see. I became increasingly certain that I had better find a way to either change the weather or get out of the storm.

It's not that I didn't try to reach greater depths of spiritual maturation within my own business context. But my efforts in that direction were not well received by my fellow executives and were thus short lived. It now appeared that I had reached the limits of what the corporate world could offer me.

8   A Boundary with No Lines

I freely admit that my first encounter with the old Zen anecdote of the cup of tea was completely confusing. The story, familiar to many seekers, goes like this:

A young monk, eager to be accepted as a disciple by a famous Zen master, asks to meet with him for an interview. The monk has traveled for many days on foot to reach the master. He is so excited to have finally arrived that he barely completes a quick bow before blurting out the question that has been burning in him for years: "I will do anything it takes, O Venerable One, but please, you must tell me—how can I become enlightened?"

The master says nothing; instead, he turns and signals his attendant, who nods and then returns in short order, carrying a tray with a samovar and two cups. As the master pours the tea into the first cup, the would-be disciple continues to chatter away about his experiences in meditation. It is not long before he notices that the cup is almost full—but the master is still pouring. The monk doesn't want to be impolite, so he tries to ignore this. But when the contents spill out onto the tray and then begin to overflow onto the floor and splash onto his robe, he jumps up and cries, "Master! What are you doing? Can't you see that the cup is full?"

The master looks up at the disciple as though acknowledging him for the first time and says, "This cup is *you*. What you have come to receive cannot be given, for you have no emptiness to receive it."

Whoever these Zen people were, they must have had a different sense of experience than I did. For five years, I'd been the darling of the CEO group and had taken in as much as I could, so I was definitely running on the more-is-better plan. Through this simple story, I was exposed for the first time to the concept that having too much of something could actually be an obstacle.

There came a point, however, when I started to feel the winds of change. Most of the members of the CEO group were ready to sell their interest in the companies that they had founded, and for the rest it was time to move on to something new. The dissolution of my TEC group was one of those events that clearly marked a change from one chapter to another. As the youngest in the group by some twenty years, I was one of the only CEOs whose career was still on the ascent, so at first I felt lost. But I soon realized that this turn of events had left a fissure large enough for something new to become noticeable—the sense that a truth deeper than I had been able to grasp was now available to me. All the signs were pointing to this possibility, and it lay in a domain not circumscribed by my corporate self. This spark of realization pushed up from below and ignited my passion. The eruption, seemingly in charge of itself, created the behavior of searching and seeking with an urgency like none I had ever felt.

At the time, I had been married for more than ten years, and my daughter, who was six, and my son, three years younger, were already enthusiastically along for the ride. My personal explorations, which puzzled and often exasperated almost everyone else around me, created not a ripple for my kids. The three of us were aware that we'd come from the same egg, so to speak, and we intuitively understood one another's needs. The marriage that produced Kristin and Michael was something else altogether. This union had been created immediately following my mission in Peru—and "created" is definitely the word for it. In order to give you sense of my marriage, let me take you back to the beginnings of that union.

In the Mormon Church, successful executives commonly take a three-year hiatus—often at the height of their career—and volunteer to oversee hundreds of missionaries between the ages of nineteen and twenty-one. My mission president was a gentle man in his mid-forties by the name of Elder Driggs. He and his family had arrived in Peru at the same time I did, and he remained my immediate boss throughout all my leadership assignments. All I remember from that interview is a deep, penetrating set of blue eyes looking over a pair of reading glasses and, in the kindly tone he always used with me, the words, "Alan, when you arrive home, the first thing you should pursue is to find yourself a suitable wife."

My memory of that moment is as vivid as if it were yesterday.

I responded to this directive with the same passion I applied to every other instruction that had been dispensed during my mission. Within three months of my return, I found a young lady who fit the bill. From that time on, and all throughout my meteoric ascent in the corporate world, she and I formed a perfect management team in the eyes of those who knew us. Unfortunately, this perfect pairing never extended into an especially intimate connection of any kind.

To this day, I feel sorry for my first wife. She couldn't have had any idea that the glimmer on the track that first attracted her was attached to a large train coming toward her at light speed. When the initial stirrings of my new pursuit of truth arose, it began with a need to revisit all the chapters of my life that had led up to that time. I felt it necessary to assure myself that some nugget of truth that I'd perhaps stumbled across earlier wasn't still out there somewhere, ignored or incomplete, due to my laziness or a simple wavering of attention.

This life reexamination mainly took the form of the deconstruction—or possibly the destruction—of many of the major structures that I had built to that point. Not surprisingly, the first areas that I felt needed to be probed were the relationships already present in my life—specifically, my marriage. From my wife's point of view, personal fulfillment and a search for the deeper meanings in life, while somewhat interesting, were irrelevant and could easily threaten a relationship whenever unexpected weather arose. So my wife "for time and all eternity" put me on notice that our life had better continue to look the way it always had. She had signed on as a Mormon wife and, being from Orange County, she expected us to continue to uphold the image that was the main component of such unions, which had included a climb up the corporate ladder together. It didn't take too long before this expectation became a demand that I discontinue my "searching madness" and return to what I surely must know was my rightful life. We separated, then divorced. This initiated a pattern of ultimatums, followed by dissolutions, which would continue in other areas of my life.

My earlier struggle with feeling trapped in the contradiction between concepts taught to me by others and truth based on my own direct experience had, by now, mostly disappeared. It's true that I'd had some authentic experiences in Peru and in my profession, but these were wrapped around a set of concepts or principles emphasized by others who assumed that those were the point of whatever we were doing. I had pushed aside my acute discomfort about this and replaced it with the discipline of single-focused action, subjugated to concepts that I had adopted for myself. In fact, I gave my concepts all the credit for every outcome in my life. If someone had suggested to me that experience is the driver of concept, and not the other way around, I wouldn't have known what they were talking about.

The experiential had always been calling to me, even though I didn't know what that meant, and thus had no idea how to respond. It was no surprise, then, that I pointed my new need to explore toward the conceptual realm where I was so comfortable; I couldn't imagine any other doorway into experience.

Thus began a three-year immersion into the world of books. Not just any kind of book, but those that professed to deliver deeper truths. I began by gorging myself on almost all the books that I could find on philosophy (that is, those I hadn't already read). I had a vague recollection from my childhood reading of the *Great Books* that in the world of philosophy, some of the great ones had flown close to the flame. So I began to dive into the works of the later German philosophers, including Hegel, Nietzsche, Heidegger, and even the occasional French philosopher, such as Derrida.

But it soon became evident that if I were going to find what I was looking for, I would have to go beyond readings in Western philosophy. There had to be some way to make a jump out of my tried-and-true approach of reading and collecting knowledge as *the* way to conquer anything. I was now looking for a doorway that would connect the conceptual with the experiential. It seemed to me that books on metaphysics, psychology, religion, mythology—and, especially, mysticism—would fit the bill. I became a constant visitor to the "weird section" of the metaphysical bookstores in Orange County. Their selections were fairly limited, so I soon expanded my search to the bookstores of Los Angeles and San Francisco, where materials on these subjects were more commonplace.

I was still interested in the latest developments in the corporate world, so I didn't neglect writers such as Stephen Covey and Peter Senge. But my reading expanded into all the theories of ego development I could find, *A Course in Miracles,* many of the Christian and Eastern mystics, books by assorted self-help gurus, and any material on mythology I could get my hands on, including all the writings of Joseph Campbell. I became good friends in print with luminaries such as Sri Aurobindo, J. Krishnamurti, Carlos Castaneda, Ram Dass, Louise Hay, Ken Keyes, Meister Eckhart, Thomas Merton, St. Teresa of Avila, and many others.

One of my first encounters with Eastern mysticism came via an anonymous quote: "If you need experience, go get experience." There it was again; everywhere I turned, this seemed to be the watchword. But even with all my new knowledge of spiritual subjects, that statement had no practical relationship to life as I knew it. Activities such as meditation, which I gathered would relieve this problem of the lack of direct spiritual experience, were totally out of my league. So whenever I came across this admonition, I scratched my head and continued on to the next book.

Eventually, I came across the assertion that all concepts need to be dropped in order to access the deeper truths of life. If it was difficult to grasp the supremacy of the experiential over the conceptual, you can imagine that it was out of the question for me to embrace the notion of leaving aside concepts altogether. My response was to just keep on reading—and let's pick up the pace while we're at it. Pushing harder was the way I'd dealt with everything; I couldn't see any reason why it wouldn't break something loose here. But whatever that breakthrough was to be, it had to happen in the ballpark as I defined it.

Since I knew of no major in metaphysics or mysticism, my natural next step was to enroll in a graduate program in philosophy. My business was running smoothly, so I had some time on my hands, and I saw my chance to go back to school—this time to study with no other driver than my own passion. I knew that the best philosophers had gone to great lengths to understand the nature of mystical experience, and I was equally interested in exploring the framework in which truth arises and the content of that truth. It seemed to me that these were one and the same.

Thus, at the age of thirty-five, I spent a year at Claremont Graduate School in Claremont, California, studying with my usual intensity the works of the postmodern, deconstructive philosophers. I had arrived with the suspicion that most of us live from a view of reality that we ourselves have fixed, whether consciously or unconsciously. We are so conditioned by the influences all around us that we become blind to the entire system we've set up for ourselves. When we deconstruct our assumptions, the opportunity arises for us to see alternative possibilities. Realizing that my sense of this matched the observations of the modern scholastics helped me to ground my thinking on this and other matters.

I soon found, however, that I was not a cozy fit with the process of graduate education. Many of my fellow students became my friends, and all of them were pursuing a career as philosophy professors, something I was no longer interested in doing. Unfortunately, that path and the path of someone who needs to know the truth are not the same. I constantly found myself the object of shocked disbelief on the part of both the students and the faculty. Whenever I asked a question, it was because I wanted to know the answer. I mean, I *really* wanted to know the answer. I can't tell you how many times I heard, "How will you ever get a recommendation from your professors if you continue to ask questions like that?" Most of the students felt compelled to accept the answers to their queries as those answers were given. But if I heard a response that did not satisfy me, I immediately dismissed it and asked again, this time with considerably more insistence.

I was still functioning as the senior partner of the CPA firm I'd formed years earlier, so gathering recommendations and making money in the philosophy world were not relevant for me; this freedom allowed me to leave the program a semester before completing my master's degree, with no sense of anything lost. My need for this new freedom was lost on the secretary of the Philosophy Department, who called me a year later on the dean's behalf to express their shared hope that the program's star student would return.

One day in early March of 1991, I had an appointment scheduled with a potential client in the city of Yorba Linda, only a few miles from my hometown of Corona. I was still studying at Claremont, but had enough space to see new clients whenever I needed to. That winter day was sunny and just turning warm when I rolled into the parking lot in my white Mercedes, which sported the vanity plate "THEECPA." Nobody could have mistaken my importance if they had been there to witness my arrival, but there wasn't a soul visible. Before sauntering into the waiting room of the large concrete tilt-up warehouse that housed the company office, I noticed a sign on the outside of the building that read "Osho Aloka Meditation Center." If I'd been paying more attention, perhaps I would have guessed that this would be a different type of meeting.

I immediately noticed in the corner of the small entryway a table loaded with stacks of paperbacks. What they all had in common was their author—an Indian man whose picture was on the front cover. Being in the middle of a book binge and possessing the nature of a heat-seeking Alan, I was immediately drawn to them. When my new prospect came to collect me, he found me thumbing through one; I had to drag my attention away from a lengthy passage that had my complete attention in order to greet him. I don't remember whether I even introduced myself, but I do know that the first question I asked was, "Who wrote these books?"

He responded with a grin just about as wide as his girth and pronounced a group of syllables that sounded like gibberish. In short order, I discovered that the man standing in front of me had the curious name Satyam Rich, and was from New York, of Jewish descent, and an accomplished professional pilot who had spent years in India in an ashram with the man who had written those books. After a mere ten minutes of explaining his company's dilemma and promising to send me all the documents pertinent to the task of restructuring his business, he invited me to sit with him in the meditation room that occupied, by far, the largest part of the building. We spent the next five hours sitting on pillows on the floor in a semidark room while he described his personal journey, which included his experiences in India.

As I was leaving, Rich handed me a copy of every single paperback on that table, then sent me on my way with an invitation to an event the following Sunday, which he called satsang. This was the first time I had ever heard that term. He described it as a "meeting in truth" that would include meditation, celebration, and words from the guru who had authored those books.

As soon as I arrived home, I grabbed something to eat and opened the book whose title I had found the most intriguing among the lot— *Tantra: The Supreme Understanding*. And I did a Parley P. Pratt—that is, I stayed up all night reading it. The moment I finished the first passage, I knew that I had found an access point so unique that it would make the hours spent reading the rest of it pass as quickly as a coffee break. If experience was the topic, this man wasted no time getting to the point.

The experience of the ultimate is not an experience at all—because the experiencer is lost. And when there is no experiencer, what can be said about it? Who will say it? Who will relate the experience? When there is no subject, the object also disappears—the banks disappear, only the river of experience remains. Knowledge is there, but the knower is not.[1]

In these words I found confirmation that experience is the key. I had been finally given a lead that I realized was worth following. But how? And to where? I had no idea, but I knew that wherever this would take me, I would go.

I was a little nervous about the upcoming satsang, but I had been well trained in how to deal with such feelings. Plus I had completed a fair amount of spadework by then. In my reading frenzy, I had spent many hours dissecting the various versions of transformation that were out there at the time, examining closely all the roadmaps that I could find. I was finally at the point where, both in my thinking and my behavior, I wasn't putting any limitation on how truth might appear. I had also clearly established in my own mind that the ego, and the way it is consensually defined, is at the root of how life is experienced by each individual. Thus it would have to be the ruthless focus of any self-examination, in this or any other setting. I had prepared myself intellectually and emotionally as well as I could for my next step in the process of personal transformation. All in all, I felt ready for whatever I might find.

When I stepped into the meditation room (shoes off, please!) the following Sunday, I found myself in a space whose design was about as far from that of a conference room as you can get. Maroon fabric had been draped with sweeping curves along the walls to soften the visual impact of the coarse gray cement underneath, and the carpeted floor was scattered with pillows and cushions of various sizes, shapes, and color patterns. There wasn't much else in the space besides an elderly upright piano that hugged one side of a wall, opposite the floor-to-ceiling windows that let in the bright sunlight.

It immediately became apparent that this wasn't anything remotely like a gathering of corporate personalities; most everyone was dressed as though they had been invited to a gypsy banquet in the middle of Turkey. This odd collection of individuals—from twenty-somethings all the way up to those who looked like they were their eighties—were milling about the room, talking, laughing, and letting out the occasional squeal from the press of a full-body hug.

But neither the kaleidoscopic outfits nor the hippie decor nor the lack of anything that could be called decorum could distract me from my quest to discover whether what these people were about could assuage my thirst. I picked out a cushion that looked reasonably comfortable and a wall to lean against that would give me the best strategic view of the room and its inhabitants. Rich hadn't arrived yet, and no one spoke to me, so I just sat and waited. Then someone yelled out that the meditation was about to start, which mostly everyone ignored. Eventually, the noise died down as people found their places on the floor and arranged themselves in what I'd come to know is called the lotus posture. I squirmed around on my cushion until I was as comfortable as I could manage with my legs intertwined like gnarled tree roots, and I waited some more. No one seemed to be in a hurry. Starting on schedule was obviously not a priority here.

Rich had told me that following the meditation, we would move right into listening to a tape of one of the many discourses that Osho had given over the years. This was initially confusing at first, for two reasons. First, because I didn't know at the time that virtually all of Osho's books were not actually written; they are edited transcriptions of his talks, about half of which are translations of his discourses in Hindi. And second, because the author's name on the covers of the books I'd been scarfing down all week sounded completely different. It turns out that the man called Bhagwan Shree Rajneesh had changed his name to Osho several years before he had died—"left the body," as these people called it—in January 1990, so the two were one and the same, after all.

I was somewhat interested in seeing what the meditation would be like, but what I was really there for was to hear what this man had to say. During the last stage of the meditation, the quiet in the room was palpable, in glaring contrast to the state of my mind. I had never been in an atmosphere permeated with such deep stillness. After a few minutes, a soft river of words, shaped by an Indian accent daring to be understood, began to seep into the silence.

As I heard Osho describe the journey of the ego, my acute listening for concept melted away into a state of undivided experience, one that embraced everything, including the concept of the ego that I had been listening so carefully for. Osho's accent and the occasional oddly placed word were no problem. It was as if my grandfather himself were speaking to me. I immediately knew that this man *knew*.

But let me be clear. It wasn't Osho's understanding of the ego that was so transfixing; it was the fact that his own experience of the ego was opened to me in that moment. An entirely new possibility for accessing the seeker's insights that I had accumulated as intellectual understanding became available.

His words, and the experience that was so obviously behind them, were further evidence for me that the land beyond concept is unknown. The fact that it is unknown was obviously considered by this Indian guru to be a normal feature of life. I immediately understood that walking in the unknown would be the main feature of my future transformation.

This could be called my first mystical moment. During my all-nighter earlier that week, I'd had my first experience of being so totally consumed by what I was reading that the book and I became one and the same. But what happened as I listened to Osho speak was an experience arising from silent sound that lived far below the clackety-clack of a mind careening down the tracks. To bring that mind into silence was one thing; to have that mind swallowed whole was another. I had crossed what had seemed to be a boundary, but looking back, I saw no lines. The piece that I had imagined to be missing had been there all along. I had been thrown into the endless space of experience.

From that moment on, and to this day, even seeing this man in any of the many photographs taken of him during his lifetime brings tears to my eyes. The love I feel can scarcely be contained, even in this large Irish body that people identify as being me. Before I even finished hearing my first Osho discourse, I knew that I needed to go to India and "get experience."

It should become obvious to anyone who thinks about it for a while that language and concepts do not precede direct experience. It must be the case that some caveman picked up a rock and examined it far ahead of the need to call it a rock. It was only when he needed to explain to his caveman neighbor what he had found and which sizes could be used to bonk which animals that its name became relevant. And so it is in all human affairs.

However, in our modern world, we often lose sight of the primacy of direct experience. We immerse ourselves in making up names, formulating concepts, and producing all the reading materials, courses of study, and institutions of learning needed to contain and explain what we have fabricated. As we learn to intellectually process information, we attach our life energy to that process, and concept becomes the most alive experience available to us. We attach our actual sense of experience—of our very being—to the concepts themselves, often to the point of separating ourselves from one another and going to war because we are so violently attached to our own cultures, political views, and religious beliefs. But those thoughts were not in operation as I sat there, unmoving, in the afterglow of a first moment. I was aware that the other people in the room were getting up and moving around, but I had no need to interact with them. I was perfectly content just to be.

The CPA who had arrived in his trademark golf shirt and Docksiders looked the same on the outside as when he walked in the door, but within a couple of hours, he had been altered internally beyond recognition, even to himself. He finally could say that he had some understanding—even if just barely—of this thing called experience. My cup was certainly still way too full, but it had emptied just enough for my entire search to shift. Whatever was happening here, I knew I needed more of the same. And now I had the address of this Indian man!

Within two hours of arriving at my office the following day, I made all the arrangements to fly to Bombay on the first of May, which was less than two months away. The only reason I didn't choose an earlier date is because I felt responsible to make myself available during tax season, always our busiest time.

I had downsized my practice after my divorce, but it was still thriving, and I had a wonderful partner whom I had trained myself. The last time I had taken a personal vacation for more than three days had been about ten years earlier, so I knew before making my announcement that morning that she wouldn't object on that score. But running off to India to spend time at an ashram, with no specified return date, was hardly normal behavior for a senior executive of a prestigious CPA firm.

Toward the end of the day, my partner sought me out for the details. After I had notified her of my plan that morning, she'd spent most of the day in shock, and had only now pulled herself together to ask the necessary questions in the orderly manner to which she was accustomed. But her disbelief won out over her discipline, so this is how it came out:

BUSINESS PARTNER: But what will you be *doing* there?

ALAN: I don't really know. But I know that I've gotta go.

BUSINESS PARTNER: Well, how long will you be gone?

ALAN: I don't know that either. Several weeks, at least. But it could be several months.

At this, she turned pale. Trying her best to manage her emotions and retain a professional posture, she had a go at smiling in my direction, but it didn't work. I could tell she had been chewing all day long on something that was causing her angst beyond the anticipation of having to shoulder more responsibility in my absence.

ALAN: Okay, spit it out. What is it?

BUSINESS PARTNER: [*with a look of panicked desperation that defies description*] What will happen if you decide to come back months from now, and we have gone bankrupt?

ALAN: Then we will have the experience of going bankrupt.

It was then that I realized I had passed into an expanded version of what behavior looked like for my ego. Having finally been introduced by Osho into the unknown, I was now watching it make its initial appearances in the domains of my life that were formerly defined and dominated by the Alan who was a walking paragon of structure and strategy. I was beginning to see the first cracks in the self-mastery that I had worked so hard to crystallize. My intuitive, experiential self, which was no longer being completely screened through a verbal or conceptual filter, was starting to make the decisions. Powerful ones. I could tell that I was already far beyond the point where my intellect would mount any meaningful resistance.

On my return some months later, I could see the glimmerings of a power larger than my self-mastered ego manifesting at my firm. Far from being bankrupt, the company had actually flourished during my absence. This result could only lead me to ask, "How important could I be if, in all the time I was away, I wasn't needed at all?"

And that is how I began the life of an active seeker.

Osholandia

One of the first anecdotes I heard soon after my arrival in the ashram was a favorite of Osho's that he loved to repeat. In this story, he likened the life of the seeker to that of a man who has willingly jumped off a cliff and is hurtling through the air. As he plunges past his fellow travelers, he hears their voices echoing in the canyons as they call out to him, "So far, so good . . ." It was in this spirit that I stepped off into the space known as that of the seeker.

After awakening, it is not difficult to speak about the jagged walk through broken glass by which the ego has crossed from the known into the unknown. Entering into the experiences that lead to this point is an entirely different matter. Many call this entry "the beginning of the return to the Self"; others call it "setting out on the journey of personal transformation." But on the runway, no markers are apparent. My newly honed awareness of the possibilities of spiritual experience, and my usual hair-trigger readiness to respond to anything I might encounter, prepared me to plunge into what was waiting for me over the next few months. But as my plane lifted off above the Los Angeles smog, I felt a surge of apprehension common to those who enter into an experience with no idea of what is to come.

It makes sense that anyone raised in a culture solidly built on conceptual structures would find it a challenge to begin living on the slippery platform of experience as it arises moment to moment. In the years that followed the initial opening that Osho's words carved out in me, I would witness many who could not make that transition. They would arrive at the ashram expecting some great transformation to happen and leave bewildered not long afterward. For some, the atmosphere was altogether too alien; for others, the experiences that lie behind what is affectionately called the Gateless Gate of the ashram simply jettisoned them. A good chunk of me wished to avoid experiences that evoked emotional pain; in this I was no different from anyone else. But the fire within me was not to be denied, and even as vulnerability mixed with fear burned through my belly as I approached this new land, I understood that there would be no detours.

If the process I was embarking on was completely beyond anything that could be called familiar, at least I had found the perfect place to play this new game. Not that it seemed that way from the get-go. Before her wheels even touched down in Bombay, the plane was filled with an odor unlike any I have ever encountered. It was the smell of India in its hot season—old tires, body odor, and fragrant incense all rolled into the glue of early morning humidity. Friends who had spent time there had carefully coached me on what I could expect when I first arrived, but not even their most detailed portrayals could have described the actual assault on the senses of a country like India.

As my driver steered his taxi into the traffic outside the airport, I was struck by the realization that I had never seen so many different vehicles in motion in one place, much less this close to one another. I was an old hand at navigating the L.A.-area freeways and city streets overburdened with way too much traffic, but this was something else altogether. Bicycles, taxis, motorcycles and scooters, motorized rickshaws, battered cars with mismatched colors and parts, and trucks of every size and description were jockeying for position on the road. None of these vehicles appeared to be in a lane of traffic, or obeying any traffic rules, or even aware of anyone else on the road. The occasional oxcart, small pack of ragged canines, or desultory cow would enter the fray, adding to the chaos.

Just about every vehicle I saw had more people stuffed into it or piled on top of it than you would think is humanly possible. At any moment,

I expected one of the women or children clinging to papa atop some frail bicycle to tumble to the ground with a scream that would be barely audible in the soundtrack of shouts, incessant car horns, squealing tires, klaxons demanding right of way. This cacophony competed with the shrill tones of what I later came to know was Bollywood music, which seemed to be pouring out from every direction.

One would think that living in Peru in the early seventies would have prepared me for the lack of amenities as well as the poverty that I would witness. But India is not a place that yields to preparation by experiencing any other country. It was three in the morning as we made our way to Dadar train station, and I couldn't help but notice that most everyone I saw was sleeping either on top of a car or on a sidewalk. As we drove through the night, the driver proudly announced that Bombay was populated by some forty million people, twenty million of whom were homeless and slept exactly in this manner.

I had been instructed to commandeer another taxi to take me to Pune once I reached Dadar. This last leg of the journey turned out to be four hours of misery, bumping over a pothole-filled dirt road. Still, it wouldn't be fair to describe my first exposure to India as an exercise in unmitigated suffering. Despite the obvious poverty and pain, I couldn't help but see beauty everywhere. Especially the colors. The deep hues of the Indian landscape seem to grow out from the ground and live themselves as part of the decor. Intermingled with all the smells, they surge and seethe around you. And I can tell you that a taxi jaunt past the Bombay flower stands enlivens the senses in a way that only the newest designer drug can approach.

I strained to absorb the immensity and grace of the country, but at some point simply relaxed into it and let it roll over me in waves. The early-morning sounds of India—roosters crowing the day awake, the lowing of water buffalo on the move, and the splash of water from battered tin cans as people crouched in the streets for their morning bath— were my welcome committee when I at last arrived at my destination. It was about seven by then, and the mists hung over the fields as farmers hauled huge metal milk cans to market. How these skinny men managed to keep those cans balanced on the unruly tree boughs that they had cut and hung over their shoulders was beyond me.

My friends had cautioned me to spend a day or two resting in my hotel room before jumping into action. I could see their point, since my trip had taken more than thirty hours end to end, and I was now in a time zone twelve and a half hours different from that of California. The taxi driver looked as wilted as I did by the time we arrived at the hotel and, grateful to him for having delivered me alive, I was happy to hand over my fare in Monopoly money—this time in the form of Indian rupees.

I dropped my suitcase on the bed, took a shower and, after pulling some fresh clothes out of my bag and tossing it in a corner, decided to attempt to follow the instructions I had been given. I dutifully lay down, closed my eyes, and waited. Maybe it was the oppressive heat or the coarse woolen blankets shedding fibers that no human with eczema could stand, but my lapse into obeying instructions didn't last. By seven forty-five, I was standing at the gates of the ashram, straining to get in.

Eventually, I heard the muffled slap of approaching footsteps, followed by the scrape and groan of the gates being opened from the inside. The face of a sleepy Indian in a loose, ankle-length maroon robe and faded rubber flip-flops fell into a gentle smile. He must have gathered from my expression that I was a new arrival, so he said, "Welcome home" and led me straight to the ashram's welcome center. Here the ever-eager Alan was told that he would need to arrange for an HIV test, the results of which would not be sent over until the next morning at eight. Like it or not, I was forced to take at least one day to rest before being allowed to wander freely in the ashram. My friends back home had told me that this would be the drill, so as hungry as I was to begin the pursuit, I made the best of it.

After getting the green light the following morning, I hightailed it over to the place where newcomers are advised about which groups or individual sessions would be most appropriate to sign up for. As I walked up the few steps to the wraparound porch of the old house that contained the Multiversity offices, a lanky, almost frail, man in flowing black robes sat strumming a guitar, seemingly without a care in the world. He looked up over his instrument and, waving me toward a seat across from him, asked in a soft but unmistakable English accent whether I minded hearing a tune.

ALAN: I would love to listen to your guitar solo, but I am here to get something done and I have no time to spare.

COUNSELOR: When did you get to the ashram?

ALAN: Yesterday at seven a.m.

COUNSELOR: Don't you think you should take some time to really arrive?

ALAN: [looking all around and then straight back at him] I'm right here, and I've arrived.

Before I reproduce what followed, I should point out that many of my friends had told me that the point of being a seeker is to become enlightened. Now I didn't know anything about enlightenment other than the things that my friends had tried to say about it and the concepts I had gleaned from the books I'd read on Eastern spirituality. Since the term sounded good to me, however, I had easily acquired the use of it. So the rest of the conversation went something like this:

COUNSELOR: Tell me, what are you here to do?

ALAN: I am here to get enlightened.

COUNSELOR: And how do you see that happening?

ALAN: I figured that you could give me a list—in order—of things that I need to do. I will start at the top and do them one at a time, and when I finish the last one, I will be enlightened.

He chuckled, then spent some moments in silence, looking out over the fragrant garden that surrounded us as he considered his next tack.

COUNSELOR: I don't suppose I could get you to wait a few days, just to settle in.

ALAN: I feel quite settled as I am.

Much like in the story of the coconut pie, I only knew one way of doing things: Make a list, execute, eat the pie. So although I knew that my ego-definition was about to be thrown onto the examination table, I still felt compelled to employ my tried-and-true recipe for self-mastery.

During this entire exchange, I had been sitting on the front edge of my chair, looking more like a lion in wait for his prey than a person seeking wise counsel, so I doubt that Mr. Black Robe concurred with this report of my inner state. But that's how I normally look when I am ready to fall onto my next assignment. To this day, anyone in a similar situation with me cannot escape the sense of impending launch of the projectile seated across from them.

My British minstrel must have concluded that whatever he prescribed for me had better keep my full attention. And that is how I ended up spending the next five days in the Primal encounter group, completely absorbed in excavating my childhood conditioning.

It is extremely difficult to describe the nature of an Eastern spiritual journey. But it borders on the impossible to explain how Osho, as a modern-day master and guru, elevated and expanded this path. The basis of commune life as I experienced it back then was an attitude of willingness on the part of those who lived or visited there to look at their own unconscious conditioning. Much of this inner work was accomplished through the psychotherapeutic processes used in programs lasting from three to sixty days, which were carried out by one of the ever-changing schools under the umbrella of what was called the Multiversity.

These groups had originally been modeled after the techniques from popular movements that had emerged in the sixties and seventies, such as Gestalt Therapy, Rebirthing, Bioenergetics, Primal Scream, the Fischer-Hoffman process (before it became simply The Hoffman Process), and various encounter groups. Their approach was not based on a map of concepts presented as the ultimate objective in a pursuit of knowledge. Various maps were embedded in the processes, to be sure, but we were handling live ammunition. Every group demanded that we exercise awareness in order to see our conditionings as they arose each moment in interaction with others who were just as blind to theirs as we were to our own, but also just as motivated to uncover them. This was real, on-the-ground experience.

Osho was well known for his teaching that sexual energy can be used as a path to understanding how we have unconsciously limited one of our most essential energies. The community was, in fact, sexually open, but the point was to help you see your conditioned fears and limitations. So when there was a good reason for it, nudity was used within groups as a natural expression of that understanding. Of course, this area of his work is generally judged and criticized heavily.

But even though the ashram may have looked to outsiders to be the spiritual version of a carnival tent or the fleshpots of Egypt, I found it to be a place where sincere seekers bent on using the opportunity to look at themselves could take advantage of the huge variety of means for doing just that. Osho had created the entire ashram experience as an open canvas for people to engage the limits of their own boundaries in every direction. And as people's conditionings were being brought to light, their awareness was further cultivated through the meditations available every day in the ashram. The two aspects of self-reflection and discovery, of examination and meditation, were always intertwined.

Whatever the particular focus of the inner work, I always felt that the magic of the process was in our willingness to challenge one another to reexamine the stories that keep us limited. This confrontational style, both inside and outside of the groups, came with its own set of fluid rules that were uncomfortable and unwieldy. It was quite normal to be challenged at any point and at any time by any person in the ashram to "take a look at" whatever trips your ego was generating.

So although therapy groups, sessions, and a variety of active and silent meditations were major components of this process of self-discovery, the experience of ashram life extended beyond any particular activity. Even if you were taking a break after an extended period of intense inner work, you were woven into the atmosphere of exploration through whatever you were doing. Having a job in the ashram was its own kind of group process, and simply being part of the larger community kept you soaked in the juices of Osho's vision for "a new man and a new humanity" as it played out in every area of ashram life and in your own personal relationships, romantic and otherwise.

Some people, it's true, came with no other intention than to hang out and have a good time. And in the permissive atmosphere of the ashram, everything from passionate sex to simple, natural affection was right at one's fingertips. But the invitation that permeated the entire atmosphere was continuously extended to everyone who walked through those gates: to explore the boundaries imposed by family, society, religion, and culture, and to do so outside the reach of their influence.

The experiential nature of the groups opened me up for a quantum breakthrough in my spiritual quest. These processes became my focus for the next two months, extending into the next two years as I went back and forth between Pune and California, the lion's share of my time being spent at the ashram. I was lucky to have arrived well past the era of turbulence stirred up by the world press that held Osho in low esteem; the time was ripe for pure experience without any distraction by public opinion. I took groups that dealt with primal and sexual conditioning, codependency, fear, and love, plus several groups that each centered on a different meditation method, such as the witnessing experience known as *vipassana*.

At one point, I signed up for a six-day group called "Acceptance." The point of this process is to be able to embrace the shadow side of the ego—that is to say, the parts of ourselves that lurk in the unconscious and that we'd rather not see. On the first day, we were asked to identify and write down our three major unconscious traits. We dutifully set out to comply, only to be told by the group leaders that we really weren't giving our full effort—this turned out to be true—and we were sent back to the drawing board again and again over the course of the first three days. It took four exhausting days, but I finally came up with a list that felt authentic to me:

1. An unconscious habitual liar
2. Uses sexuality to dominate
3. Sees others as objects to use

I suspect that most successful businessmen—in fact, I'd say most people—engage these traits in order to succeed. But upon the recognition of a trait that no sane person would want to claim as his own, the immediate reaction from the solar plexus is to disown it. I suppose it might have been possible to duck the full force of these revelations except for what happened next.

This group had thirty-six participants, which included twenty-four women, many of whom I would have dearly loved to know better. So when it was announced that the next part of the process entailed standing on stage in front of the group and announcing our unconscious traits through the microphone, I was stunned. It only got worse when I found out that, whenever my turn came, my three revelations would be followed by a Q & A period during which I could be asked anything that anyone wanted to know about me.

Of course, I was the first participant selected to mount the platform. It wasn't until I was standing in the middle of the stage that the final instruction was given: "Before you speak, please take off all your clothes."

As I stood there that day, it was clear to me that I wasn't who I thought I was. I knew, well enough, the body that was presenting itself in the room, but the labels that had both defined and terrorized Alan up to that point no longer were my identity. Whether we label them positive or negative, they all eventually reveal themselves to be merely ornaments on a bare Christmas tree. I could sense that the tags sewn on my personality were for display purposes only. And there was no way to classify the eternal essence that we all know is there.

Yes, the emotional response to all this was almost too difficult to contain, but it was in this intensity that I had one of those moments that a seeker longs to experience: The conditioning that held together the parts of me on which I had hung the sign "Unwanted! Stay back!" simply crumbled.

As I stepped down from the platform, I found myself surrounded by three dozen pairs of arms, into the center of which I gratefully collapsed. The love and support I felt all around me coalesced into a silent, palpable presence that held me as firmly as the sturdiness of their bodies. In the timeless flow of indescribable grace that surged through the room, I could see a figure here and there melting into some man or woman who had been held at a distance because embarrassment, shyness, or judgment had been blocking the way to an authentic heart connection.

A group of human beings who had started out as strangers from very different social and cultural contexts had, without saying a word, merged in the shared sense that we were all, just for those moments, the same. In this space, I could not distinguish their hugs—or their hearts—from my own. And I had finally experienced a taste of what it was like to reclaim my shadow attributes, a process that would continue for some time to come.

10 Osholandia II

My description of the ashram might convey the flavor of a highly structured atmosphere. Although the usual daily functions—such as preparing food for the multiple restaurants and cafés on campus, running the administrative offices, cranking out the *Osho Times* newspaper in several languages, scheduling work assignments, and processing new arrivals—not to mention the coordination required for the Multiversity to operate smoothly—were efficiently done, the overall feeling was one of chaotic responsiveness. It was almost a daily ritual to show up for a certain activity, only to find it canceled and some other event organically taking its place.

But somehow or other it all worked. This is a miracle itself, considering that the ashram population which, it has been claimed, normally was four thousand to five thousand people, could swell to twenty-five thousand during the festivals held regularly throughout the year. Newcomers found out soon enough that this was a place where anything could happen.

When Osho was in the body, he enjoyed creating devices that would help awaken his followers. Through his verbal instructions—whether delivered directly or through someone he had assigned to the task—sudden changes in the ashram environment would occur when least expected. Although it happened before my time there, this is one of my favorite stories: One night, after the evening discourse was over and the restaurants had closed, the gates were locked as usual behind the last person leaving. By the time they were reopened in the morning, every building had been repainted from its former color to black. Who knows how many people it took to do the job, but it must have taken all night. Even the longtime ashram residents probably had no idea how to respond to this new version of their spiritual nest. As for me, I lived in excitement and terror that any day spent in the ashram might introduce a complete and sudden change.

It wasn't long before I realized that the fabric of the ashram, loosely knit as it was, was an extension of a wider pattern of chaos and disorganization in Indian culture. India herself was only too glad to play her part in the disorientation of a newly arrived Westerner. One day a friend of mine, Adri, decided that we should visit a traditional Hindu temple and meditate there. Now when Westerners meditate, they typically demand such things as a comfortable amount of space around them, a quiet atmosphere, and the like. But Indian conditioning does not lead one to expect a cushy meditation space with at least twelve inches between people. While you were in the ashram, whining and complaining about certain conditions in the environment might have yielded some small gains toward having it your way, but in the world outside, you took what you got.

Adri was a hardy, six-foot-ten Englishman with gently graying hair, piercing blue eyes, and a voice like God's. As a merchant marine, he had jumped ship in Panama because the prospect of living there seemed a better deal than staying confined on a boat. He had arrived in Pune by way of Sri Lanka, where he had worked for a while as a gem cutter.

This was a man of salt and spirit who was always good for an adventure. He had been in my Primal Deconditioning group, and therefore had been a witness to my platform revelations, just as I had been privy to his, creating a lifetime bond between us. I readily agreed to go with him to a temple that some friends had told us was a few miles away. As we made our way on Adri's scooter with its rubber-band engine, the air screamed with the sounds of taxis, motorcycles, roosters, and blaring TVs.

Once inside, we sat shoulder to shoulder with about fifty Indian men and women (including the requisite quantity of children) in various states of hygiene on what was yet another sweltering, humid day. Now it was the job of the cleaning ladies, at their convenience, to sweep the hall at intervals throughout the day, whether or not meditations were happening. Shortly after we began our sit, I couldn't help but hear Adri, who was seated next to me, stifling what should have been a belly laugh. Of course, I had to peek out from the corner of my eye. Today's pair of designated cleaners, each with her sari tucked up between her legs, were staring intently at something on the floor near him that had caught their attention. This would not have been worthy of note except for the fact that these ladies had parked their cleaning gear on either side of Adri—one broom per shoulder, and a dustpan apiece leaning against his right and left thighs.

Ah, yes, it was meditation time in India!

The commune itself had grown from a mere six acres in the late seventies to, by the time I arrived, thirty-two acres of beautiful gardens and buildings, along with a swimming pool, tennis courts, and Zen spaces where seekers could spend minutes or hours or an entire day undisturbed—meditating, reading, or simply breathing in the fragrance of the water lilies.

Nestled inside the spread of the ashram gardens was a meeting place covering an area that seemed to be roughly the size of an American football field. Here, in Buddha Hall, with its sturdy canvas roof, white marble floor, and mosquito netting for walls, silence and sound wove community life together in the myriad activities that happened there throughout the day. All the meditations, important meetings, and the daily morning and evening sessions of taped lectures by the master took place here.

During discourse, the deep quiet that permeated the hall made the experience of listening to Osho's words—on everything from early philosophy, to Eastern and Western psychology, to virtually every religious and spiritual tradition on the planet, to politics and social culture, and a list of other subjects too lengthy to include here—even more profound. If you found yourself out in the gardens and walkways nearby at lecture time, your ears could easily pick up the melody of Osho's accent as his words floated by. The music for Sufi or African dance or for the various stages of Dynamic, Kundalini, Nataraj, or any of the other hour-long meditations created by Osho would become so familiar that it became part of your inner soundtrack.

Amidst all of this, the master was still powerfully present, though he had left his body some months before I arrived at the ashram. I felt a palpable bond with him, and it had the same delicious flavor as the connection I had with Grandpa. In Osho I had found a man whose personality didn't fit the mold of what one normally assumes a religious wise man should be. His style was that of a ruthless surgeon who demanded no less than the cutting away of all that blocks the way to a life of pure consciousness. And he had no fear when it came to challenging any and all assumptions that create life as we know it. Memories of times spent with my grandfather often came to mind as I sat in discourse and listened to Osho speak. As it was with my grandfather, no topic was considered sacrosanct or out of bounds. I had found our third musketeer: Osho was one of us!

Osho was reflected into life as a looking glass in which anyone who chose to could see their own reflection, and I knew from my first morning at the ashram that I wanted to look in that mirror every chance I could, for as long as I could. Indeed, I had fallen into a love affair of the highest order. Embedded in that love was the invitation to become initiated into sannyas, which is to say, into a master-disciple relationship that is also an entry into an entirely new way of being. In the East, it has been recognized down the ages that becoming enlightened requires having a master who has already blazed the trail. To become one of Osho's sannyasins means that one has chosen to engage in a personal journey with him as sage and master, in search of the authentic self we all share.

Sannyas is a well-known phenomenon in several Eastern spiritual traditions. In his inimitable way of using everything as a device, Osho, still called Bhagwan Shree Rajneesh, had lifted the term "sannyasin" from Indian religious culture. The Buddha had called his disciples sannyasins some twenty-five hundred years earlier. But in the minds of the traditionalists, this Rajneesh was a charlatan who committed a sacrilege in doing the same, for the ancient, venerated forms of sannyas looked nothing like the neo-sannyas of his creation. Hindu and Buddhist sannyasins have historically committed to an ascetic, repressive lifestyle of strict practices, often as wandering beggars, or sadhus. The majority of the people I met in the Pune commune had already taken sannyas either at the ashram or in one of the many Osho meditation centers throughout the world, and it was immediately clear to me that these individuals were anything but ascetics.

Many people agonize and analyze their way through the decision of whether to take sannyas; for some, it takes years to arrive at a yes. There was never any decision for me to make. The moment I heard about sannyas, I wanted it. When I'd been told about it back in California, an urgent *yes* had exploded into my awareness. But I kept my cool, hiding the intensity of my desire. I was afraid that, like my red hatchet, this, too, could be whisked away from my grasp. Once again, I was close to something that meant everything to me, and you had to be on your toes.

Even so, as with everything else that mattered to me, I wanted it yesterday. I hadn't been in the ashram for even a week when I set about convincing the therapists leading my Primal group to give me permission to leave for an hour to go for the required interview for that week's initiation ceremony, which would be happening two days later. All I knew about it was that the majority of people who ask for sannyas opt to receive a new name, which is given, along with a mala—a necklace of 108 beads and a locket with Osho's picture—during a celebration called sannyas initiation. These were held each Saturday morning at nine.

To my surprise, the interview was not the bore-right-into-your-sore-spots screening process that I had imagined it might be. The Australian woman who interviewed me seemed to intuit immediately that it was the right time for me to take this step. In her warm, disarming way, she found my heart, and my fear melted away. I was going to get my wish.

I woke up that next Saturday at five-thirty, and the India that I had fallen in love with so quickly was present in all its resplendence to greet me. It was monsoon season, when it is not unusual to have ten inches or more of rain during any given day, with humidity at an intensity I have experienced nowhere else on Earth. But a day of rain followed by a night when the moon hangs golden within the clouds gives birth to a morning fit for Tolkien's hobbits. It was on such a morning, with the mist rising from the dirt roads and mixing with the smoke from small cooking fires every few hundred yards, that I made my way under the disappearing moon to the ashram from my flat five blocks away.

I spent the hours before the ceremony in the lush ashram gardens, where I would often take my books and sit tucked away in a corner with the lily pads, pretending that I was with Buddha himself. As the hour approached for the ceremony, I took my time walking down the path that led toward Buddha Hall, taking in the fragrance of the flowers and trees that flanked both sides. Through the netting that surrounded the hall, I could see the musicians, facilitators, and what looked like about a hundred other sannyasins readying themselves for the event. I was already awash in sweat and, as is always the case in high humidity and heat, my face was the same bright red that had earned me the nickname "Tomato Face" early in life. But I was absorbed in the beauty of my surroundings, and my body was on autopilot; I had no cares.

I was greeted as I entered the hall and then directed to sit in a special section with all the others who would be taking sannyas that day. About ten sannyasins in black robes, with strands of crystals and beads adorning their necks, sat at the front. Arranged carefully before them atop a colorful Indian tapestry were various stones and crystals, plus the malas that would be given to each new sannyasin. My fellow travelers in their maroon robes—the dress code for everyone except those whose roles were distinguished by the contrasting black—sat on their legless meditation chairs or stood in excited anticipation as they watched those who were at the edge of the moment, preparing to take their dive. It was as if all the older kids were hanging out poolside and waiting for someone to shout, "Okay, all you new kids—into the water!" They wanted to hear—and feel—the same splash as when they themselves had jumped in weeks, years, or decades before.

And then it began. Everyone in the hall started to sing, clap, and sway as the music slowly built in intensity. The musicians were pouring their hearts out as though it were the last performance of their lives. When my name was called, my pounding heart, sweating hands, and all the rest of me somehow made it to the front. On the way up, I caught sight of my Australian interviewer, so by the time I got there, I felt reassured by the love that was holding me in the shine of her eyes.

As soon as I sat down, I was completely taken by the power of the light that surged like electricity from the marble floor to the crown of my head. I couldn't help myself—my arms raised themselves and my head tilted upward toward the heavens. I let the tears fall as the musicians, in perfect sync with my energy, drove themselves to a joyous frenzy in a perfectly rhythmic unmeasured cadence. The entire hall seemed to lift into the air, as though carried on wings of energy unseen yet unmistakably present.

I have no idea how long this went on, but when the music finally subsided, I felt that I had crossed the invisible threshold into a world that I loved sight unseen. Then, silence. Like a horse pulling at the reins, I strained forward, every muscle alert, as though I could get myself a few nose-lengths closer to hearing my new name spoken out loud. When the woman giving me sannyas finally pronounced it, I could feel the soft center of that moment whisper it back to me: "Anand Darpan." These two Sanskrit words, she said, translate as "blissful reflection" or "mirror of bliss."

I had come a long way, and this name was now etched on the doorway to my new path. I loved both the sound and the meaning of it. And my friends knew how much I loved to hear it. Whenever I strolled through the gardens or down the main ashram drag, the sound of it wafting through the air as someone called out to me was pure pleasure. To this day, I receive it with a tenderness akin to the falling petals of a flower.

My American friends immediately shortened it to "Darps," as only Americans do. And although this name seems entirely unsuited for the hot-wired businessman that most people assume me to be, it is easy to find that blissful reflection if one only scratches the surface.

It was only in looking back that I realized I had not felt any boundaries separating those of us in the throng that day; a snapshot that I have of the moment pictures the contrast of "me" being witnessed by "them," which was not at all my experience. As soon as that mala was placed around my neck and the new name was mine, I was one with everyone who was in that hall and, in some way, with anyone who had ever become Osho's disciple. Gone was the "otherness" I had felt when I first arrived. I had actually dubbed the people at the ashram "UFOs," since the topic of extraterrestrial life on Earth merited serious discussion here, unlike on my stifled corporate planet. Taking sannyas sent me orbiting in the ethers beyond the world of conference rooms and corporateness that had come to feel so familiar to me, and so manageable. I would happily remain in this new orbit throughout my next two years in the ashram and during the four to five months annually that I spent there for some five years after that.

The grace that made itself my friend during this ritual of commitment extended all throughout this extended period. My first year witnessed a completely green seeker being thrown into the churning waters of an unfamiliar ocean and plowing through them with single-pointed purpose, and never without total effort. Because of this, I was accepted very quickly as a real seeker. It didn't take long for the second phase to kick in. Toward the end of my first round of inner work, I was invited to assist as a therapist in some of the group processes.

When I jumped into the required trainings, I found those experiences to be as challenging and exciting as when my focus had been on my own issues. Within eight months of my arrival, I started to facilitate for several of the Multiversity groups, including Primal Deconditioning, Tantra, and Chakra Energy. I once estimated that by the end of my last stint in Pune, I had spent some two thousand hours either as a participant or a facilitator in various process groups. (Who else but a CPA, a good friend pointed out, would have bothered to count?)

As I moved from the wonderment of experiences that were primarily for my own benefit into the world of being a mentor and therapist, I began to find a new stability under my feet. Whatever it is that engaged me so completely in my own internal examination spilled over into a leadership role for the benefit of others. This expanding embrace felt natural and easy, even in this crazy setting, and my encounters with the unknown continued at an increasing voltage. The same current that had provided the energy for my own process now swelled to twice its original power, rushing through me and tripping the switch that lowered the gangplank so others could follow me on board.

I could not resist the pull that kept me in this flow. It was common for ashramites to take "time off" to hang out on the beaches in Goa, about seven and a half hours south, or to visit the Taj Mahal or the magnificent temples of Khajuraho. I had no time for that; I knew that the energy I was steeped in could not be found just anywhere. (Osho once joked that if you want to know what sightseeing is like, simply buy some picture postcards.)

I can honestly say that there have been many times when life has lived me, and not the reverse. My years in Pune were just such a time. There was no doubt that the ashram was my home. I quickly became part of a motley crew that hardly qualified as a coherent group except for the fact that we kept our hearts in the same place. For me, Osho's mosaic was a picture of incredible happiness and freedom overlaid with intense fear and distress.

"Batman is on the superhighway to enlightenment," Adri would say, and we would both laugh. But the laser-focus warrior who had gone all out to vie for a small red hatchet had come full circle and found a place for the balancing energy of the heart. Externally, the ashram was that place, but it was a reflection of the heart that was being birthed within the grown man that I had become. As a child, I had responded to the call to climb the mountain of achievement for the sake of achievement itself. Now, standing at the bottom of that mountain once again, the adult warrior intuitively understood that his heart for all he loved was to be his precious cargo. This was life's first invitation to cross the boundary from warrior to lover and sage.

When I left the ashram, I was still a seeker, still hungry to grab on to anything that life, in its emerging divinity, would throw my way. But as I continued plummeting through the air toward the abyss, the unknown felt much friendlier, and everything in me reverberated with a sannyasin's knowing: So far, so good.

11 Stalking the Corporate Ashram

In the robust examination of my early childhood and the conditionings that constituted my ego, I had uncovered some of the mechanics of ego formation and seen through the self-limiting definitions of Alan that I had created in order to survive. It had been a time of pain and pleasure as well as a celebration of new beginnings. However, on the other side of the coin from beginnings is the space held for endings. Existence had granted me visit after visit to the highest peaks of aliveness. Learning how to witness the particular form of endings called death would now take me into the deepest valleys.

If you believe that you are your body, then its extinction is the most serious of issues. Facing that issue is a seeker's final exam, and my time to take that test had come. I wasn't facing my own death at that point, but the truth is that all deaths are part of your own demise, for whenever you encounter death, the ego cannot help but know that yours is on the way. By that point, I already knew that I am more than a body-mind; but that didn't mean I was home free. You could say that I was an expanded, but still identified, doer—or, as Osho described it, that I had gone from being merely unconscious to being blissfully unconscious! So, like a child who still needs training wheels on his bike, I had yet to test myself on the open sidewalk. In my continuing quest to face my own attachments and identifications in real time, I would have to make my way through the clarity and pain that would emerge and subside as I witnessed the deaths of the two people I had been closest to since childhood. And so it began, in the wobbly fashion one would expect.

At the end of my first year in India, in February of 1992, I returned home to Southern California to find my beloved grandfather entering his last days. Many times, little children freeze in memory the positive image of the people they love most. Just as often, they are surprised to find out much later that this freeze-frame doesn't match the person they have cherished. When it came to my grandfather, that was not the case. Here I was, approaching the ripe old age of forty, and my grandfather was still that beautiful, white-haired wizard with the magic smile that reached out and held his adoring grandson.

Before I left for India the first time, he had asked me why I had decided to take what seemed to be a detour. "Grandpa," I said, "I'm going because I want to finish the stories you told me as I sat on your knee when I was little." He, the man of twinkling eyes, winked at me and said, "Well, then, before you go, we'd better make sure that you remember them all." And so, in our Puff-the-Magic-Dragon way, we transported ourselves back to 1956, and Grandpa recounted every one of those tales again. At the end of the last story, which he told with an extra helping of tenderness on the day before I flew off, we sat together and cried. It is the only time I remember my grandpa with tears on his face. A grandfather and his still-devoted grandson swore a pact that those tears would be ours alone.

For my Primal group at the ashram, we had all been asked to bring a teddy bear that reminded us of the one we'd had as children. During my first shopping trip one stifling afternoon, on dusty, chaotic MG Road in Pune, I was lucky to find one just like mine. As instructed, I carried that stuffed bear for weeks, both during and outside the group, while I encountered the pieces of my childhood conditioning as they surfaced. Now, as my grandfather lay dying in a hospital room, I pulled a chair over from the corner and sat at his feet with that teddy bear, just wanting to be in Grandpa's presence. Night and day, I was given the gift of his non-stop attention, and he was given mine. It must have been something to enter that room and witness the three-day last communion of our little twosome. Whenever the doctors or nurses came in to announce the end of visiting hours, they saw me close to my grandpa's bed, clutching my bear, and quietly left the room. This all happened in the silence of our togetherness; Grandpa could still open his eyes and look at me, but he had stopped talking just prior to my arrival.

So it was déjà vu when, in less than a year after my grandpa's passing, I returned to my beloved California to be with my mother, who was in the throes of ovarian cancer. The news of her diagnosis had come to me in October 1992, through my youngest brother, Russell, who had spent some months with me in India. By late December, I was at my mother's side. Not wanting to miss the final moments of her life, I stayed close to her for the six months before she died. During that time, she invited me to ask her anything I wanted to know. She knew that our family had never spoken of my real father, choosing to pretend that he never existed, and I believe that she wanted to rectify what she thought had probably been a painful experience for me. But I never felt the need to have that conversation with her or, for that matter, about any other aspect of my upbringing. Why would I want to rake through the coals of my personal history when we could simply be together? Instead, I spent her final weeks simply sitting with her, in the bedroom that had been my sister's during my youth, enjoying the presence that she was.

As she lay with her head propped against multiple pillows, we revisited the little world that she and I had created when it was just the two of us. If only you could have been there with us. It was like the old days. When I was a teenager, we would sit close to one another on the drab hallway carpet until two or three in the morning, just talking. Now our union took flight from where we had left off. She would talk of literature, her lifelong love. And I would wax eloquent on philosophy and my time in India. The man that I had become pleased her, and she drank her fill. Her main regret was that she'd be leaving behind her grandchildren, and mine was that I was about to lose my first coconspirator in my earliest adventures. Right up to the end, her bright blue eyes, always ready for the next daring feat, never dulled.

My final days with Mom were a gift that any son would treasure. The end of our story was as perfectly timed as a mama bird's pushing her progeny out of the nest. When my mother left, Existence released me further into the journey that she was proud I had embarked upon.

About six months after my Mom died, I started hearing from some friends about a new emotional-release process that was being offered in San Diego. It was called the "Miracle of Love Intensive." This nine-day process, which began each morning at six-thirty and formally ended at nine at night—followed by a couple of hours of homework—focused on the emotions that accompany identification. It couldn't have arrived in my world at better time. I had chosen not to return to India as originally planned, so I was free to dive in.

I entered the Intensive trusting the same energy that I had experienced in the presence of my grandpa from the time I was very young. The space that the group provided opened up a huge conduit for all of the emotion that I had either skillfully evaded in my previous forty years or else hadn't quite moved through in earlier work. At one point I remember sitting in a local restaurant with my companions, an untouched plate of food in front of me, crying uncontrollably for more than an hour. From the looks I got from assorted servers and patrons, I could only assume that captains of industry didn't go there often to cry.

As the days progressed, I became aware that, one by one, I was losing my attachments. Bathing in the energy of love supported the device of kicking down the doors of certain types of identification that would never haunt me again. The flavor of this work was emotional to the core. The freedom I experienced by the end of those nine days I later recognized as a temporary moment of awakening. After that, my day-to-day experience started to shift; larger swaths of awakened consciousness were arising, and with greater frequency. I became even more attentive to my process, if that were possible.

The following year, I volunteered to staff the Intensive, and ended up helping to facilitate ten of them over the next year. I was subsequently invited to install and cofacilitate the process in India (now recast and renamed "Path of Love" by the Multiversity), along with three other facilitators. So I spent chunks of the following three or four years continuing my inner work. But the impulse also arose to put a foot back into my old world. I now found myself looking for challenges that would strengthen my self-witnessing no matter where and how my life would continue to unfold.

At that point, an event occurred that provided the perfect opportunity to do just that. After my mother's death, I had met a lovely woman named Justine and married her in 1995. She accompanied me to India and then through the processes in California. But we had never needed to organize our lives around being full-time parents. That was about to change. My son, Michael, now twelve years old, decided that he no longer wanted to be with his mother and asked if he could come live with me and my wife. We had not expected this, but reality has its own way of reconfiguring your game plan. So Justine and I willingly became exactly what we had never anticipated being—full-on parents.

It is a testament to the release of identifications that had begun in me that this major shift in our lifestyle occurred without any drama. Before that, I had resisted—or at least chafed at—any structures or responsibilities that might block my ascent in important areas of my life. I had always been happiest when making my way unimpeded through the corporate world or the inner journey. But now the call to be a father and live in a more traditional way did not trouble me. What many people might consider a compromise was turned on its head, and I threw myself into the life of a householder. In fact, I embraced it as an unexpected opportunity for the identifications that still might be hidden beneath the surface of my ego to be reflected back to me.

Many times over the years, people have asked me if I regretted spending so much time away from my children while I was in India. The answer is yes. When I was at the ashram, I often thought of my kids, with whom

I have always been very close. But it was this closeness and the hope of developing my capacity to father them in a more meaningful way that made it possible for me to be away from them for those stretches of time. All three of us now know that the clarity that emerged out of my transformational journey accomplished exactly that.

Luckily, I had already begun to entertain the idea of working again in the corporate world. While I lived in India, and in the years that followed, I had maintained enough tax work to support my lifestyle. But my profile had been significantly reduced in the corporate circles that I had previously inhabited. Now, new possibilities for reentering business began to arise; but this time, I knew that they would need to be personally nourishing and resonate with my life journey. Once that intention was clear, I watched as executives who wanted me to work with them in more of an advisory role found their way to me without any effort on my part. This was a timely discovery because, in addition to having my son to caretake, my fourteen-year-old daughter, though she continued to live with her mother, also needed my stable presence in her life.

Over the next few years, I would be a CFO, a CEO, and an advisor to several start-up companies. In each case, I was asked to help break through a paralysis in their growth curve and provide the leadership components that would move these organizations beyond their current identity and performance levels. I soon found that my expanded capacity to identify the motivating factors for spiritual seekers easily translated into understanding the motivations of those who sought to create or expand their businesses. I was startled to see that the companies I touched met their challenges and accomplished their goals in an entirely new way.

The change in my overall client composition made itself increasingly apparent. In earlier years, I had developed my corporate style by attracting individuals and organizations that expected good output coupled with a cultivated outer image. I was now attracting clients who all had one thing in common: They viewed every aspect of their lives, including their corporate activities, as an occasion to stretch and develop themselves.

My own style of work was undergoing a radical shift to match that need. Most of my meetings had a flavor of the impromptu that seemed to defy any fixed agenda and often flowed into completely different areas than originally planned. But each movement would occur as an organic response to whatever needs I could sense arising, moment to moment. In the past, I had prepared myself to "belong in the room"; now I would simply show up for appointments and the needed insights manifested on their own. The field in which solutions made themselves apparent to anyone who was available to them opened effortlessly. Production, marketing, distribution, personnel, management—all the standard elements of business would compose and recompose themselves without any sense of anyone being driven by anxiety or the need to prove oneself. New ideas and creative perspectives regularly configured themselves in front of our eyes.

Suddenly, it penetrated my intellect that there was no reason to flee the playing field that I had judged as not worthy or capable of generating personal transformation and awakening. I had made the mistake that so many of us do: *I tried to run from the man I really was by judging my sphere of influence as unfit for the spiritual pilgrimage.* As soon as I realized that the corporate environment was the perfect arena for inner work as well as for outer achievement, my old environment quickly repopulated itself with leaders who had the same inner drive as I did. They were asking me to deliver the wisdom that would solve their problems and, in the bargain, we were unwittingly discovering a working vision of a corporate ashram. From the outside, everything looked the same: Deals were made, companies were bought and sold, the phones still got answered. But our takeaways now included the development of a robust inner life, pursued with the same gusto as reaching for a position high on the Fortune 500 list.

I began to understand that I was not just a merger/acquisition guy with an appetite for spirituality on the side. I had metamorphosed into a leader in organizational development with a strong foundation in the spiritual world. I had read just about every book on the theory of leadership and presence in the corporate world. As a foot soldier who had marched with the armies of corporate minions wielding their diagrams, models, and rules, I had been able to talk the talk and walk the walk. But it was only through being molded by life itself that I realized that, although these books had been useful to me in certain ways, almost all of them are distant reflections of real leadership. Authentic leadership is the stuff that lives in the emergence of actual experience. That is to say, leaders are real people, and leadership manuals generally consist of theoretical abstractions about those people and their organizations. Not only did I recognize that the tracks leading to Awakened Leadership run beyond self-mastery; now I was actually riding the train.

This reminded me of my grandfather recounting Plato's story about the men in the cave: A fire in a cave projects a set of shadows on the wall. The shadows of the objects, not the objects themselves, are all that the men in the cave ever get to see, so they live their lives never witnessing the reality that is the substratum of what they are perceiving. Just so, leadership concepts projected by PowerPoint onto a screen are not the same as what leaders actually do.

It was during this time that I met Jerry Skillett. Jerry was a Kansas kid who had cut his business teeth in the parking industry. He was the brightest visionary I had ever met, and we immediately became fast friends. In our first meeting, he covered an entire conference table with blank butcher paper and proceded to fill it with details of a navigation plan that Captain Kirk himself couldn't follow. Jerry needed a financial resource in his company who could hold a structure that was always in movement. I was that guy. We cofounded a digital imagery company that we named 24–7 digital, which created an innovative web-based delivery system that would later become the standard for imagery distribution.

Jerry had an approach to execution that was much different from my own. For every meeting he attended, I am sure that he spent double the conference time preparing for it. By that point, I had become so comfortable with my intuitive approach that while Jerry was hitting the books, I would often sit by with a latte and a good novel. After a while, though, I experienced a pang of guilt; was I carrying my weight here? So for our next meeting, I pulled out all the stops and spent long hours studying all the materials I could find on the investors and companies that would be attending.

I must confess that my performance at this gathering might have been my worst ever. My opinion was confirmed when, on the way out the door, Jerry turned to me and said, "Alan, please don't ever prepare for a meeting again—leave that part to me." Jerry and I often laugh at this story because it is so obvious that my value in any meeting is in the sense of presence felt by those around me. I had become a container for those who simply needed me to be there—and out of which successful transactions could arise. Since that day, I have never looked back and have always trusted in the perfection of whatever happens once I step inside that door.

It was in the midst of this return to the traditional, yet now vastly expanded, life in the corporate world that my own spiritual search was moving closer to its final chapter. My wife told me about a man named Prasad, who was conducting satsangs in the San Diego area. It turned out that he had facilitated at a Northern California community many of the same processes that were available at Osho's ashram. After that, he had spent time with H. W. L. Poonja—affectionately known as Papaji—who was a follower of a sage named Ramana Maharshi, and a revered saint in his own right. Over the next year, I became a regular at the meetings that Prasad held twice a week. I had never heard such clarity about all the processes I had undergone. The more I sat with Prasad, the more my capacity as a seeker seemed to be growing. I was at the edge of being able to intellectually hold the understanding of nonduality. At times, I had experienced the dissolution of my personal boundaries; now I was being introduced to a concept that didn't include those boundaries, and I was at a stage where I could finally grok it.

Much of my previous inner work had occurred in an environment of swirling contradictions that, for all its immediacy and aliveness, didn't give rise to the kind of intellectual clarity that could open the doorway to the actual experience of awakening. Or perhaps it had just not been my time. In any case, I didn't give it much thought; I just kept going and did whatever was in front of me. Over the prior seven years, I had been asked to surrender to a series of processes, each of which had netted significant results but none of which gave me access to a unified theory of everything. Now the momentum of the process itself began to assemble all of the disparate energies I had experienced and weave them into the clarity of a living understanding. I had been furiously paddling for years with my head down, hoping to simply stay above water. Finally, I was swimming in a new pool of wisdom that supported and contained the entirety of who I am. The last thing left for this spiritual swimmer was to lift his head and see.

As I attended these satsangs, I absorbed everything I could of what is referred to as *advaita*, or the direct path. I became familiar with the names of Nisargadatta Maharaj and Robert Adams, who, along with Ramana Maharshi, formed the backbone of this lineage. It wasn't long before I was introduced to the books of Ramesh Balsekar, beginning with the one titled *Your Head in the Tiger's Mouth*. With the same blinding speed and certainty I had experienced when reading Osho for the first time, it became as clear as day—this man *knows*. I immediately set myself to devour everything I could find by this living sage. Apparently, he had been giving satsangs in his home every day for the better part of twenty years. In the course of that time, some fifteen books had been produced. To my delight, I found out that he was still living in Mumbai.

Now this was not your stereotypical Indian guru who had spent his life in a cave. Ramesh was an educated man. He had graduated from the London School of Economics and had risen up the ranks to become the CEO of the Bank of India. At sixty-five, he retired and, as is the custom in Indian culture, entered into the stage of life dedicated to one's inner growth. Almost immediately, he ran across a poor man in Mumbai named Nisargadatta Maharaj. In 1973, Nisargadatta had set the spiritual world on its head with the publication of *I Am That*. On the heels of its success, many Westerners poured in to hear Nisargadatta at his morning and night gatherings. I can only imagine the experience of being present at one of these.

This humble sage had spent his life up to that point as a maker of Indian cigarettes known as beedies. These foul little things are manufactured in the red light district of Mumbai—which one has to see to believe. Picture a cramped meeting room on the third floor of a dilapidated building in the city's worst section, with tobacco smoke wafting up through the floor boards into the room day and night. It was here that Ramesh soon found himself translating for Nisargadatta, who spoke only Indian dialects, for the foreigners who crowded into that tiny space. In the course of time, Ramesh experienced his own awakening. And in the days before the death of his beloved Nisargadatta in 1981, Ramesh was instructed to begin to hold his own satsangs.

I was intrigued to discover that the way Ramesh used words to express his experiences and his knowing was almost identical to mine. I would read a sentence and realize that I could have written it in exactly the same way. More important, I found emerging from the pages of his writings a uniting factor for my own life. For it was here that the assertion that all the activities we undertake are one and the same finally stuck. There is no real difference between cutting vegetables with your spouse in the kitchen, walking the dogs, playing golf on vacation, or making a multimillion-dollar deal.

From that perspective, it became clear that transformation is not the exclusive property of seekers and gurus; it is every bit as embedded in any other domain. The old paradigm of the separation of the spiritual and the so-called worldly was revealed for what it is—completely bogus. In our global culture of advanced technology, the awakened coaches of leadership authenticity are the equivalent of the saints and sages sought after by eager seekers on the path of ultimate truth.

I continued to consume all I could find in this exciting new domain called nonduality; at the same time, I was being shaped by a new understanding about the world of business for which I had so much love. Corporate dynamos continued to seek me out because they were hungry to experience themselves in ways that are not customary in corporate settings. I was being called into the vanguard of the new paradigm; however, I was not quite finished with my own process. I had been delivered to the ultimate finishing school and was now in the hands of yet another father who was a lion of a man, as all the rest had been. In the spirit of Ramana Maharshi, Ramesh Balsekar was to take me the rest of the way. The full-grown tiger in the cover photo of Ramesh's book, looking straight out at me with uncompromising eyes, put me on notice: My head was already in the tiger's mouth. All that was left was to wait and see when those jaws would snap shut.

12 The Flight of the Cargoless Plane

From the occasional to the permanent. This would be the next segment of my journey. Even though I had accumulated a large number of experiential placeholders for awakening, I found myself still engaged in "seeker's energy"—always looking, looking, looking for what still remained unknown. Sometimes a direct realization of truth unexpectedly blossomed out of a pointer. At other times, I simply held these pointers as conceptual understandings. My identity with a thing called Alan did slip out of place from time to time, but it still had some solidity.

It was in this phase of receding identification that I found myself some ten-plus years after beginning my personal search. The trek had taken me through shelves of books, down dusty roads in India, and back to the high-rise conference rooms where I had gone from a pup to a big dog. I felt grateful that my experiences of expansion made it easier for me to live with less turbulence and more peace; but although my misery index did not register at its former seismic levels, I still felt an internal sense of bondage. The cover on the seeker's hole had opened to allow in occasional sunlight, but I was still pushing to find my way out. Eventually, I accepted that this might be the situation in which I would always find myself. In this state of relaxation, one more event was yet to happen.

November 11, 1999. It's hard to forget a day numbered 11111999. I was driving up the freeway to Century City to attend a meeting with Jerry Skillett and some investors who might back our still-new 24–7 digital, Inc. As luck would have it, a well-known actor in Hollywood was so enthused about our proposal that he had asked his attorney to meet with us to review our plan. This attorney was housed on the fortieth floor of the skyscraper inside the Century City complex. If you know anything about that hulking tower of glass, you know that a conference with someone on the fortieth floor means that you have hit a home run.

So there I was, weaving my way on a typical mindless drive on the infamous 405. The stereo was on, and my attention moved back and forth toward whatever was drawing it along the way. The only unusual feature of the ride was that the traffic northbound was moving nicely. Then, in an instant, the world turned itself on its head. There was no longer an individual named Alan who stood independent within the world and apart from its functioning. In fact, the sense arose that the entire manifested world included this Alan—and all of what was in that world could be felt at one time. People always ask me what that felt like. It's like the sweet relief you would feel if you'd been walking for miles with a pebble in your shoe and suddenly it was removed.

All I had ever known was the effort that I was continuously generating to take charge of and live each moment. Now I could clearly see that the moment itself was bigger than I was; my attempts to control it had been, and always would be, futile. The heavy weight of identification had been lifted from me; I flew like a cargoless plane that never knew he had any cargo to begin with. In a word, I was free. A new thought occurred to me: I was no longer living the moment; rather, *I was being lived into the moment*. My hands still knew when to turn the steering wheel, my eyes could detect the most efficient means to maneuver from lane to lane, and my brain continued to register thousands of inputs and translate them into correct action. For all intents and purposes, you could say that Alan was driving his car. But the felt experience was that the part of my prior functioning that assumed it was performing these actions had completely disappeared. What took its place was the sense of an open field in which everything was happening on its own. Whatever was occurring had a profundity that was as light as a feather, and it was clear that it only could be arising from a much larger pool of awareness than my ego had formerly occupied.

A half hour later, I pulled into the cement bunker that we call a parking structure and took my ticket from the clock machine, like any other driver. After finding a spot and parking my car, I walked into the marble lobby of the skyscraper, greeted Jerry in the manner that we were both accustomed to, dutifully punched the "up" button for the elevator, watched as the door opened, stepped into the box, pressed the little square with the correct number, and arrived at our floor. My actions were like those of any other person on their way to a meeting. Jerry and I then entered the conference room with its long wooden table, typical high-backed chairs, and ubiquitous water pitcher surrounded by crystal glasses, and we proceeded to negotiate an investment on the order of several million dollars. All of me was present except for the part that believed it needed to conduct my affairs. There was no efforting and no sense of being a self trying to get an agenda met by some other, separate selves on the opposite side of the table.

When the meeting was over, I said my good-byes, reversed my course, and navigated home, where I was greeted as usual by my wife. There must have been a cockeyed smile on my face, because she immediately knew that something was different. In words that I am sure made no sense to her, I tried to describe the shift that had just occurred. Eventually, I realized that underneath her genuine curiosity and reasonable questions was a concern that she might not know how to relate to this husband of hers, who was conspicuously not the same man who had walked out the door that morning. I definitely had compassion for her predicament. I chuckled, the kind we always share when she needs to know it will all be okay. "Babe," I said, "it can't be any tougher than it's been up till now!" We both laughed and then went into the kitchen to cook dinner.

My good wife had done me the favor of opening the door to the understanding that I will always appear to others as they construct me to be. In the world of ego and linguistics, all I can share are pointers toward a felt experience that can never be fully communicated. As the weeks and months passed, I watched with great interest, and no little amusement, as not only my wife but also everyone else in my world tried to recalibrate their definitions and perceptions of me as an ego. This thing that we call ego was only a small piece of the whole that I now knew myself to be. It was no longer possible to identify myself with the former, limited definition of Alan, which I now understood to be merely the steppingstone to who I really am. To its great relief, the ego no longer had to strain under the weight of trying to hold together the functioning of my world.

Now you can imagine that taking a warrior personality, melting it into the entirety of what is, and removing the illusion of doership might create some mental confusion. Luckily, it was easily seen that this mental confusion was also simply part of what was arising. The ego, which had located itself in space and time within my body so many years before, was now revealed as being merely a concept that allows functioning to occur within reality as we normally identify it. Since that time, whatever is occurring is no longer happening to me. Instead, the concept "Alan" continuously arises within "all that is"—and the experience of that arising has no location, for it is not within space and time.

It would be normal to ask at this point what the difference was between this awakening event and all of the moments along the way that only had the flavor of awakened consciousness. The answer is that all of those prior events had a beginning and an end. Due to their temporary, transitory nature, Ramesh designated these as "free samples." (He had once joked that the term was his marketing contribution to the world of spirituality.) And what did these endings consist of? Each time, the mind would once again reestablish itself, and I would return to being a separate ego within all that surrounded it. Another way to say the same thing is that the sense of being a subject in a subject/object world disappeared for a while—for me, that meant anywhere from two minutes to two weeks—but this disappearance would end with the arising of the subject, the ego-defined self, once again.

I often say that the ego operates in exactly the same way as an addict does. From years of being conditioned, it develops a felt sense that attracts it to the dramas within which it plays the starring role. This is much like the experience of taking drugs. In the beginning, the ego gets a wonderful high. Of course, that begins to subside over time, so our conditioning drives the ego to keep coming back for more helpings of drama stew, hoping that it will keep being delivered, piled high and piping hot. And when the plate comes back empty, or close to empty, the ego—like all addicts—cannot help but go back one more time, still craving the fullest plate it can get. During the long period when the free samples were becoming more delicious and started to last longer, I kept returning to the addict's seat at the banquet table of turbulent drama. But at the moment of awakening, I realized that I would never need to pull up a chair to that table again.

How had I reached this point? The mind had, in essence, been fasting. That is to say, over time, the ego had been receiving fewer and fewer meals from the simmering pots of high drama. Without any conceptual wrangling, I simply arrived at the recognition that peace, as boring as it might seem to the ego, is the natural condition of human consciousness. With that realization, the high of being an ego on center stage no longer was irresistible. My identification had shifted to no place and no thing. The body-mind called Alan was still completely involved in the events around him, but there was nobody left who had the capacity to fixate on any particular aspect of these events. Thoughts still arose, as they always had and still do, but since there was no ego structure to support them, they would simply recede when they found no place to nest.

I now felt the rigid skin-boundaries of my old self sloughing off, with no new tough exterior to replace it. Over the years, I had been repeatedly told, "All there is is consciousness." Now I understood this completely. I had become—in fact, I always had been—part of all that is happening, and all of it is happening within me. I could have said that I was in the flow, except that the flow and I were the same thing. No longer stuck in identification with all the *Sturm und Drang*, I had become the container in which it all takes place.

From this perspective—and that term isn't even accurate because it implies a fixed positionality that no longer held any meaning for me—the layer of chaos beneath the stability that the ego likes to pretend is there became more than my friend; it became me. Like a championship surfer who has become so skilled that she easily maintains perfect balance on continuously shifting waves, a seeker is no longer afraid of drowning in the surf of unpredictable experience that cannot be controlled. She has come to understand that the stuff of life is extracted from the chaos of manifestation. Instead of denying its presence, she enters into it. And in this relaxed communion with the unknown, she is aware that, once on her board, she can cut through the waves without thinking about how she does it, enjoying every effortless movement. What's more, she no longer has to chase that abstract ideal called the perfect wave. Now, every wave is understood to be perfect in its own way.

During my sannyas initiation back in the ashram in India, I had touched on this awareness of the unknown that churns below the surface, so it was not unfamiliar. But now I understood why the bubbling, roiling activity of the ego continues inexorably until the moment of awakening. There is no choice. Until that moment, you can only deal with your periodic submergence in the chaos, and surrender as best you can to the flip-flop of moving in and out of those free samples. These occur serendipitously, but only the permanent installation of consciousness, free from identification with the ego, always guarantees the perfect ride with no fear of falling off the board.

It was late in 2005 when Ramesh Balsekar, the big wave that had originally carried me out to sea, swept me into his physical presence. You might wonder why it took six years from the time of awakening to be washed ashore and arrive at his feet. I could point out this or that circumstance, but the truth is that there was no particular reason; it simply happened when it was time.

I remember waking up on the first morning after my arrival in Mumbai that October. I had reserved a room at my favorite hotel, which was some thirty minutes from Ramesh's flat. Most people would hate the prospect of embroiling themselves for a half an hour every morning and afternoon in the insanity called Mumbai traffic, but I relished the idea of experiencing India again at my favorite, early morning hour. I gladly secured the services of a rickshaw driver, who would take me to and from Ramesh's each day. Memories of the flower stalls and train stations that had been my introduction to India a decade and a half earlier swirled among the sights, smells, and sounds around me. I felt the same keyed-up anticipation as when I had approached the ashram gate for the first time. I was finally going to see Ramesh in the flesh. But now there was no work to do and no seeker to do it.

Ramesh lived in one of the nicer, but not too fancy, parts of the city. His flat was near a famous temple named for the Hindu goddess Lakshmi, and I happened to arrive in Mumbai in the midst of a nine-day celebration being held there. Women wearing their best saris could be seen streaming for half a mile from multiple directions toward the temple. Lakshmi was their goddess, and they had dressed so beautifully for her that morning that an average bystander might conclude that Mother India herself had chosen their colors and tied the ribbons in their hair.

It was customary for those who attended the daily nine o'clock meeting with Ramesh to arrive about half an hour early to have tea at a café nearby. Afterward, everyone would troop across the street to his flat, where a disciple named Murthy would inquire if you had just arrived. If you were a first-timer, he would ask where you were from and what you did for a living and then offer to seat you directly across from Ramesh once you got inside. This was a trick, for as soon as a victim of Murthy's inquisition sat down some four feet from Ramesh, a microphone would be attached to his or her clothing, and Ramesh would ask his first question.

It was in this situation that I found myself that first morning. Those of us who had gathered for tea walked over to Ramesh's flat, which was in a typical Indian apartment building, and made our way upstairs. I felt safer climbing the three flights up than taking a chance on the elevator with its clattering fold-across metal gate. All the way up, I could hear blaring out from inside the elevator the Lambada, a song made famous in 1989 by a French group called Koama, which someone must have thought needed to be endlessly repeated. When I reached his flat and folded aside another iron-crocodile security gate, an ordinary wooden door with the name "Balsekar" beckoned me to open and enter into his drawing room, where Ramesh preferred to hold satsang. This tiny space held twelve people at most, but an overflow living room had space for another forty.

As I sat, cross-legged, in the first row, Ramesh gazed across the intimate gap between us, and a small smile pushed itself onto his face. Ramesh was a towering presence, but his body was only five feet tall and must have weighed in at about a hundred pounds. He was always dressed in typical Indian attire. To the average American, he must have looked for all the world like a cross between a laundry delivery man and a pirate. On his thin frame was draped a plain linen, long-sleeved, collarless white shirt, which was basically shapeless and without decoration. His white tie-up pants were reminiscent of those worn by my pirate heroes. I watched as Ramesh—still spry at age ninety—jumped into his seat like a mischievous child, his pants billowing like sails around those thin legs of his. At other times, he seemed more like a leprechaun, and I found myself thinking that if there ever were a search in Mumbai for such a creature, Ramesh would have been relieved of his Lucky Charms.

RAMESH: What in the world are you doing here?

ALAN: I am just here to be with you.

We sat for a minute or two, absorbed in the fullness of a silence that had no content. A gesture from him indicated that nothing needed to be discussed; his eyes, sharp as a hawk's, saw no ego-quarry, so he merely said, "Well, fair is fair; let's find someone with a real question!"

And then he continued on, inquiring of each new visitor where he or she had come from, their age, and what they did for a living. He then asked if they had a question. I never have been quite sure why he did that, since no matter what was asked, he would respond with whatever struck him in the moment. He could, however, in fine corporate fashion, shape whatever he wanted to communicate into a response that was perfectly tailored to the query at hand. After about an hour and a half, the meeting finished with the singing of *bhajans*. These Indian devotional songs had been the joy of his mother, and they were sung at the end of every satsang until the day he left the body in 2009.

After the last mismatched notes sung by our seekers' choir faded, I stood around in his small drawing room visiting with the others, and soon I felt a small tug on my sleeve. I looked down from my six-foot, two-inch frame to see Ramesh's brown eyes looking up at me with child-like delight. In his quiet, accented voice, which carried deep warmth, he invited me to return later for a cup of tea. I immediately accepted. That afternoon, we had the first of our many discussions about current events and economic theory. Ramesh, who swam so effortlessly in the nonconceptual, would joyfully veer into the pool of ideas and concepts, which he loved as much as the boundaryless space of emptiness. We would also tell and retell our favorite stories. Like me, he never seemed to tire of hearing and recounting these over and over again. It was just like being with Grandpa.

In addition to our daily chats, I continued to sit in Ramesh's presence each morning with the other visitors. I always encountered the same rarified yet intimate atmosphere of satsang, where ego-shattering wisdom did the tango with awareness on the dance floor where these encounters took place.

One morning about a week after I arrived, I noticed a burly, gray-haired man at the entrance of Ramesh's flat. He looked lost and seemed unable to communicate with anyone present. I immediately recognized the Spanish dialect in which he was speaking. When this fellow attempted to speak to Ramesh, the inevitable occurred, since Indian English and

Argentinian Spanish have no intersection point. I was chosen to be the traffic cop who negotiated the exchange between them because I spoke Spanish as easily as English. But my strengths were Mormon mission terminology and business lingo, not the subtle language of advaitic non-dualism. Still, I set about dutifully translating every word as best I could.

When I looked around the room, I noticed that everybody was in on the joke of this unlikely trio. The diminutive Indian guru, the rugged, bearded dockworker from Buenos Aires, and some big, Irish-red gringo from Southern California had been cast in this scene for the comedy *Tres Amigos*, produced in the best Bollywood tradition. With Ramesh, depth never was sacrificed for humor, and humor never was sacrificed to depth.

Eventually, Ramesh told me that I should find my way to hold satsangs. I couldn't picture myself doing that, but he didn't seem to harbor any hesitation on my behalf. And, like everything else, when it was time, it would happen without effort on my part.

As one would expect, my relationship with Ramesh was much different than my connection to Osho. First of all, they each began at different points along my journey. Although I never met Osho while he was in the body, it could hardly have mattered. I felt for him an intense personal love identical to that for my grandfather. With Ramesh, there weren't two of us to be in love. There was only love itself, inside of which we appeared as the body-minds that had manifested as Alan and Ramesh in this life.

When I describe the relationships of my early days, it is important to relate the particulars of each participant in order to understand the nature of the connection. However, when love is the dance floor and life shakes and grooves as it must, the résumé of each dancer needn't be known. Why would one bother? It is obvious, even to the youngest child, that dancing is dancing. Yes, each individual reflects his own uniqueness, but neither party needs to pretend that love extends like a glue-rope between two egos when they are, in fact, one. It was in this space that Ramesh and I met as simple placeholders for the one being that we are. Our moves could be observed, but our dance created itself. When nothing meets nothing, there is only nothing . . . but that nothing is all there is. Which reminds me of an old Sufi tale . . .

In the days of small kingdoms, a great festival is being held to celebrate the king's birthday, and all the ministers and courtiers are gathered at the palace. Each attendee is shown to his or her place according to position or status and, of course, there is a throne on a raised platform for the king. The chief minister, in all his finery, is standing at the bottom of the stairs leading up to the platform, waiting for the king to arrive so the beginning of the festivities can be announced. In comes a Sufi mystic dressed in rags. He walks right past the minister, climbs up the stairs, goes straight to the throne and, to the horror of the chief minister, sits down.

MINISTER: What do you think you are doing?

SUFI: I'm just sitting here.

MINISTER: You aren't even the chief minister—and you think you can sit on the king's throne?

SUFI: I'm more than the chief minister.

MINISTER: Well, certainly you are not the king!

SUFI: No, I'm not the king. I am more than that.

MINISTER: [guffaws] Don't tell me you're the emperor!

SUFI: No, not the emperor. I am more than that.

MINISTER: [trying to save face, he turns to sarcasm] Oh, so you must be the Prophet Muhammed.

SUFI: No, I'm not the Prophet. I'm more than that.

MINISTER: So you think you are God?

SUFI: No, I'm not God. I'm more than that.

MINISTER: [sputtering] But . . . but . . . there's nothing more than God!

SUFI: You are right! I am . . . nothing.

It is difficult for seekers to comprehend what the experience of being nothing is like, so perhaps another metaphor will serve as a more accessible pointer to what occurs when all ego-identification disappears.

From the time that my ego-identity first started to form, I was hard at work creating the outline of Alan E. Shelton. Only through experiencing the falling away of the white dust that formed that outline on the chalkboard of life did I understand that the outline and the chalk dust are inseparable—in fact, they are the same thing. Not only that—in drawing what I had thought to be myself, I had conveniently forgotten that the board was there. Once the ego no longer bound me to the bright white outline of self, I dissolved like magic to become the board itself. Now that I am the board, I hold all of the stick figures that appear on it. This is the authentic experience of what is called holding space. But no effort is needed for the holding to occur. In the experience of awakening, I finally recognized that the contents of life are all in their rightful place; they always have been, and always will be. I am that place.

And the truth is . . . so are you.

⚡ INTERMISSION ⚡

In one sense, the stories of my life can be viewed as snapshots of the various stages of adult maturation. Now it is time to encapsulate those stages and place them in a more orderly sequence. This approach will give you another vantage point on your own process. But it seems fitting to take a brief interlude before we launch into the final six chapters of this book, which lean toward the conceptual and may strike you as—should we say it?—more academic. Lest we fall under that spell of seriousness, it is important to remember the lightness and humor of our trail ride thus far. Hence the following lyrics, written by my good friend Brad Cahill for an unpublished song entitled "The Redneck Enlightened Rodeo." So sidle up to your own imaginary saloon bar and ask for a cold shot of your favorite cowboy beverage. Then sit back and enjoy . . . but don't fall off the barstool!

The Redneck Enlightened Rodeo

I was mindin' my own business
When suddenly an IS-ness hopped inside o' my head
I thought I was lost
Or had a brain holocaust
Oh baby, I thought I was dead

I was sittin' on my tractor
When that nuclear reactor went off inside my brain
Then—heavens above!
There wasn't nothin' left of
That me that went down the drain

Now it's the Redneck Enlightened Rodeo wherever I go
Just the Redneck Enlightened Rodeo bo dodeo doh
Now everywhere I go
Everything I see
Everyone I talk to is One (and only me)
It's the Redneck Enlightened Rodeo wherever I go
Just the Redneck Enlightened Rodeo bo dodeo doh

My baby thought I lost it
The day I got accosted by two guys wearin' white coats
They said, "Boy, we had enough
Of your enlightenment stuff
'Cause, buddy, you're rockin' the boat"

Then I flashed back to my tractor
And that nuclear reactor and said, "Boys, ain't nobody here
Better get your butts on home
And get your boss on the phone
And tell him I done disappeared!"

So baby, don't get excited
And don't cause a riot
'Cause the writin's right here on the wall
I'm at the Redneck Enlightened Rodeo and havin' a ball!

It's just the Redneck Enlightened Rodeo
And baby, that's all!

13 Ego Maintenance 101

Some of my fondest early memories are of watching black-and-white movies on TV. I would sit for hours in front of one of those squat little boxes with the big tubes inside, which were nothing less than marvels back in the fifties. My favorite films featured swashbuckling pirates, played by actors such as Errol Flynn and the star I was named after, Alan Ladd. If you remember, these larger-than-life characters would often stand on the bow of their ship and gaze through a spyglass out into the distance. A spyglass is quite useful for seeing a small part of a panorama in the most concentrated format. But if you want to view the horizon from east to west all at once, or the expanse between the water and the heavens, a spyglass won't be of much help. The activity itself emphasizes the viewing party and the selected visual patch.

It would be interesting to interview the man or woman required to live an entire life as it is perceived through a spyglass. I am sure that whatever they would report to you, it would be with the self-assurance that all of reality is represented within the little circle that forms the boundary around what they can see.

The development of the ego is based on this very principle. A child comes into the world without any sense of boundaries between himself and anything else. There are no horizons in his world of exciting smells, tastes, sensations, and emotions. But the actors that surround the infant, spearheaded by Mom and Dad, recognize that he must develop an efficient means for navigating the world, so a transmission of the concepts and experiences needed to establish an ego-identity is donated by them. The good news is that this allows the child to fit his self-definition within the tiny, circumscribed world of objects, places, events, and other beings that populate his experience. The bad news is that this limited viewing style becomes locked in and the child's ego follows suit.

We live in a world where this ego, once it is birthed into existence in childhood, is pumped up to the most concentrated potency possible. And we believe that this is normal and necessary. The child contributes her part to ego creation by intuiting which survival strategies will work best in her environment. Above all, she wants to be safe and loved. This is natural, but the problem is that the attachment to those who are perceived to be the source of all safety and love is based on the assumption that there are separate objects out there that the ego must depend on and cling to in order to maintain its very existence.

It is fortunate that, after we become disconnected from our early-childhood experiences of unitive consciousness, our deeper intuition knows that something is amiss, for this knowing is the dormant seed of seeking that may germinate later in life. On the other hand, that seed may be so deeply buried that it never breaks through the hard crust of our unawareness. Even if it tries, it may be smothered by our constant compulsion to act as this supposed separate self. The subject-object relationship and resulting dependencies remain the core of self-identity from childhood into adulthood. If we live that way long enough, the walls of our own egos become so highly fortified that we cannot find a way out of the defended castle of self that we have built. This is what it means to live in bondage.

When the ego-designed coping strategies of childhood no longer work, suffering abounds. For most people, the initial attempts to relieve this suffering focus on trying to manipulate conditions in the external world. That usually means trying to change other people, collect more toys or power, or lasso one's own self into submission to whatever we think we must do or become to achieve our goals. In addition, we keep regrinding the lens of our spyglass and spraying Windex on it in dizzying amounts, all in the name of self-mastery. Relatively few of us have the insight that the transformation required is primarily an inside job.

Even if we come to that realization and make the commitment to doing inner work, it's far from simple. If we only had to deal with the psychology of the human developmental process, then we could—if we had sufficient persistence and determination—unwind its effects, and the whole panorama of reality beyond a limited ego-view could be revealed as it actually exists. But a compounding factor arises, which perhaps is most simply described by the response of the Zen master who was once asked, "Who is this 'I' that we always speak about?" He replied, "From a Buddhist point of view, it is simply the arising and falling away of consciousness and concepts and ideas and feelings and experiences."

If this is the case, then this "I" that you think you are does not really exist. The human intellect exercises its ability to assemble all of its interpretations of what is, presses these into service as a placeholder, and then it proceeds to locate this bundle in the human body, calling it "I". We treat the ego as though it were our real self because we cannot tease out the difference between a placeholder and a real thing. Another way to say this: We have unconsciously absorbed a conglomeration of concepts and assumed them into manifested reality, where they morph into a hefty ego-maintenance manual. Page by page, we put together a set of instructions for an imagined separate self struggling to cope—often with sword in hand—with everything and everyone that does not meet our needs or seems to be acting counter to our interests.

The mind does everything it can to master playing the game of life, always competing to win that red hatchet, in one form or another—or at least save face if it can't. But many times, the outcome isn't what the mind expected, and things don't turn out as we had hoped. Then we have to keep revising our personal manuals to prevent our egos from breaking down. If we do start to fall apart, the DSM-IV manual of mental disorders—nearly a thousand pages long—can identify, label, and categorize what is wrong with us. All of this happens because we have become disconnected from the simplicity of direct knowing, and being what we know.

When I was working in the orange groves as a teenager, the superintendent of our packinghouse was a short Italian dynamo one generation removed from the Old Country. He was blessed with a love of the groves like none other. When it was necessary to teach new, young workers how to properly take care of the trees, Tony would gather those kids together and pose his favorite hypothetical-question-in-a-tale. I couldn't possibly reproduce either his lively, accented speech or the warmth of his manner, so a paraphrase will have to do:

Imagine, he would say, that you want to understand the notion of balance. And in order to do that, you decide to convene a gathering of the most intelligent scientists in the country from fields such as physics, biology, and quantum movement. Of course, in order to describe what balance is, the scientists are going to need a visual display of someone in the act of balancing something. So you pull in a local ten-year-old and his bike to be the subject of the study. Once everyone is assembled, the scientists sit down on the curb and pull out their notepads. After the young boy has ridden down the street and back, only one question is worth asking: Who among the crowd knows what balance is?

Of course, the only participant in this grand experiment who knows is the kid who rode the bicycle. The scientists would be able to produce nothing more than an observation of what it looks like from the outside when balance happens. Their contribution would be only a set of concepts that attempted to reflect what the scientists had just seen. And, as one could expect, these illustrious men and women would engage in endless disagreement, each pitching his or her particular interpretation of balance.

We had no idea what Tony was trying to tell us. So he patiently went on to explain. "I will show you how to cut, trim, and care for these trees. But when I instruct you, don't create a cutting manual in your mind. Watch how I am with each tree, but don't just copy my actions. Gradually, you will be able to feel your own way into what they need, and you will know what to do."

Every child from Corona who learned at the feet of this man could tell you that to watch him at work was to witness a love affair in motion. Tony touched each branch with care and respect, as though he were listening to the tree itself. And only the cuts that nourished the tree the most were made. "Boys," he would say, "just like that ten-year-old kid was a part of his bike, you are part of every tree in these groves." We had been raised with those trees, had lived our short lives in their presence. I saw, in a way that I couldn't have put into words, that it was our birthright to be connected to them.

It was then that I began to sense the difference between concept and experience, between observation and direct action, between imitation and true attunement. Being the boy on the bike means knowing balance, while being one of those scientists means getting all caught up in the concept of what balance is. And the love and care of those trees was a simple, direct experience that needed no interpretation.

With this understanding, we can define a concept as an intellectually assumed object that takes the place of experience. And we can now recognize that this concept called ego has the same slippery nature as all other incomplete, ambiguous, and dislocated concepts that we hold. We can also see that, due to its artificially constructed nature, any concept can be interpreted in multiple ways. Another story from a different context can help us see this:

> Two monks in training who were passionate smokers were having great difficulty sitting in meditation. When they discussed this between themselves and could not arrive at any solution, they decided to ask their respective superiors for guidance. They met the next day to compare notes.
>
> MONK #1: I asked my superior, and he was very angry that I even brought the question to him.
>
> MONK #2: That's surprising. Mine was very helpful.
>
> MONK #1: What did you ask him?

MONK #2: "Can I pray when I'm smoking?"

MONK #1: Well, what did he say?

MONK #2: He said, "Certainly, my son." What did you ask?

MONK #1: I asked whether I can smoke while I'm praying.

All human beings carry within their intellect a story about how the world is and how they themselves are. If these stories are seen as immovable, then the ego that has constructed those stories necessarily exists in exactly the same state. If we discount the fact that life is in continuous motion, we attempt to turn this moving picture into a snapshot, stuffing into a fixed and immovable concept all of the constantly changing characteristics in our little bundle of "I"—and then we act from that position. No wonder that an ego existing in a fixed state would feel bondage while living among all the other egos trapped in their own fixed states. *As long as the ego demands that everything remain fixed, the shift that allows something new to happen will remain elusive.*

You might be thinking, "So what's so terrible about living life as an ego? Everybody else is doing it! Can't all of us egos just get along?" Here's the difficulty: Because we believe that the ego is who we are, we strive and struggle to create a life for ourselves that is stable, peaceful, and fulfilling for that concept. Our agenda generally consists of getting what we want, avoiding what we don't want, and having others see us as we want to be perceived. Even if these goals were obtainable, they are based on a fraudulent concept of self. But that doesn't stop us from going after them.

Have you ever had the frustrating experience of someone just not getting who you are? Try as you might, you cannot reach that person, even with all the additions and adjustments to your self-description that you attempt to convey. Your frustration gets sharper as you keep on trying to clarify for the other who you are, but finally you realize that you will never get through, so you give up. In that moment, you are simply experiencing what is always the case: You, as a concept, are the function of the other. That is, you as an ego are nothing more or less than what others think you are, based on their projections and interpretations.

It is true that some folks will understand you better than others, but if you reflect on that, you will note that even then, you find yourself constantly making adjustments to align their picture of you more closely with your self-perception. It's just that their definitions of you started out close enough to your own that you had some hope of shaping those to match your self-image. And what about the folks who simply don't get you, no matter what you say? You have no other choice but to leave them with their version of you. For most people, that translates into having failed.

It has been noted that one definition of exasperation is a lifetime spent attempting to make yourself seen by others as you see yourself. Add to that the exertion of constantly corralling yourself into the confines of your own ego-ideal, and the whole enterprise becomes utterly exhausting. How do we manage it all?

Because the mind has the ability to categorize and separate various phenomena to help us live more or less efficiently day to day, the belief arises that some parts of life can be pursued without regard to the pieces that we either don't see or have managed to ignore. So that's what we do: Whatever doesn't fit our picture gets tossed out on its head, or we simply pretend it doesn't exist. The intellect, as it commonly develops, does not see the interwoven nature of manifestation. Much like pretending that a quilt can lose its seams and still hold together, the mind pulls what it has judged to be unwanted from the fabric of life. In each of our attempts to solve a problem, we pull on another offending thread, and sooner or later, we start to feel that our lives are unraveling. And so we try to exert even more control over our feelings, thoughts, and circumstances.

Living near the ocean, I am often surrounded by happy mariners who love to tell their boating stories. One of their favorites describes what happens the first time a newly trained navigator attempts to steer a boat with enormous sails into an oncoming wind. It seems that the rookie sailor has the tendency to clutch the wheel and try with all his might to hold it steady.

All of us who have ever steered a boat, or even a car, know that it is impossible for a vehicle to move in a straight line when we hold the wheel tightly. But this is the same approach that most of us use in relation to the ego. Instead of understanding the winds and currents of the human drama, we steer our solid-state ego directly into the turbulence ahead. In our insistence on acting like a rookie desperately trying to stay in control of the currents of living, we exist in a constant state of tension. Most of us wait until our arms are about to give out before we start to look for another way.

We also become identified with our ideas about where our ship needs to go. In experiential terms, identification occurs when a belief has been so fully absorbed that it is lived as though it were true. But if your view is limited to what is seen through the spyglass, how can you possibly know whether where you are determined to go is where you should be? As Nisargadatta Maharaj once said, "Nothing extraordinary can happen to a consciousness that knows exactly what it wants."[1]

Believing that you are your ego is the ultimate identification, but it usually takes some time before you can grapple with that, even as a concept. First you need to encounter the specific areas of identification in your life. Those who are intent on finding out how I went about doing this are usually people who have worn themselves out trying to hold their ship steady against the oncoming wind. When that didn't work, they tried blaming the weather, changing ships, or firing the crew. When nothing they did made any difference, they were finally ready to admit that they had run out of tactics and were ready for something completely new.

To those who have reached this point, I can say without hesitation: The mechanics of disidentification are the same no matter what situation you find yourself in and how long you have been stuck there. By changing the way that any particular area of experience is held by the ego—and, more fundamentally, by changing the definition of ego itself—you begin to move away from a fixed identification and into a flow that includes the activity of the entire ocean. Then life within the manifestation that you see around you arises in one piece, with yourself included in it. Rather than trying to reconstitute, rearrange, and repair the disparate parts of life that you have separated from one another, you understand that whatever is can only be an expression of the entire manifestation of beingness in movement. This rescues you from the brittle illusion that life is fixed. *The key to all transformation is to understand that nothing within manifestation is fixed or absolute.* With that understanding, you avoid becoming identified with the part and move within—and as—the whole.

So how can we arrive at that understanding? There are two interrelated ways: The first is to look into your life and work with the issues that you are most charged about, in order to bring unconscious and identified behaviors into the light of awareness. For many people, including myself, this comprises a large part of the seeker's journey. If you remember, when I arrived in India, I was immediately placed in the Primal group so that I could examine the situations and behaviors that formed my initial responses to life. This proceeded issue by issue and, as I became aware of each pattern, block, or inaccurate belief, a freedom arose that allowed me to release my tight grasp of that particular part of my personal history.

For example, after years of holding my parents accountable for my inability to create different outcomes in my life, I stopped perceiving them as offending causes in my personal story. I could see that, just like me, they had simply been living a life in which decisions were subject to conceptual understanding, which led to a lot of unconscious reactions. At that point, my judgment of Mom and Dad fell away. It was apparent from the relief I felt that these issues were unwinding and dissolving on their own as soon as I became aware that they had been the genesis of my behavior.

These types of shifts are sufficient for people whose sole agenda is to have fewer problems and more positive outcomes in their lives. But for an avid seeker, the issue-by-issue approach, by itself, does not lead all the way to awakening. Plus, it can become an endless pursuit. Behavior comprises such a wide variety of components that, like fish swarming to their daily feeding, each wriggling critter of unconscious behavior fights for its place to be the next one to reach your awareness. You can spend decades processing your personal history and still remain stuck in the ego-identification that caused the problems in the first place. So what is to be done?

The other approach advances you into the recognition that the "I" that you think you are is the same kind of concept as the issues you have faced using the first approach. That is to say, there is no one thing or object called "I". The "I" is as much a concept as "I was hurt by my father's rejection of my manhood." You may remember that Ramesh Balsekar called this sense of imagined solidity "entification"—the idea that "I think I am something." He pointed out that the body-mind exists in the world as one of an infinity of objects. You are simply one of those objects rather than being the subject "I". Our willingness to accept, even intellectually, the possibility that the ego is not a thing but rather a placeholder allows space for the experience of awakening to happen on its own.

If you constantly watch your behavior, you will be able to observe when the assumption that the "I" has authored its own existence is at play. This makes it easy to see your identification with that assumed "I". Eventually, it can be experienced that indeed this "I" is simply a concept that arises with all other concepts in manifestation. You then become aware of the natural placement of the body-mind in the arising of all existence; this allows for the identification as a small, individual "i" to reassign itself to that All. At that point, it is possible for the felt experience of the body-mind to be the natural identification of consciousness with all that is. This second approach is often called the direct method.

The Indian saint Ramana Maharshi was famous for reducing this approach into a workable device. When one of his disciples would ask him a question, his immediate response almost always was, "Who is this 'I' that wants to know?" He would then suggest that the questioner begin an inquiry by asking herself, "Who am I?" He knew that this "I" is merely a mentally constructed object. He also knew that no one had ever seen this thing called "I". He saw that when the question is continually asked, with deep sincerity, the mind eventually collapses on itself and the identification with this pseudoentity called "I" finally drops. It is this second approach that I was propelled into when I first was exposed to Ramesh. He called Ramana's "Who am I?" device a living understanding.

But most people didn't arrive at Ramana's feet ready to step into that awareness. He would often say that the seekers who came to him were like firewood. Some were so dry that one spark set them on fire. Others were only partially dry, so the ignition took some time. And then there was the waterlogged group, who needed to spend a lot of time drying out.

The secret here is to start where you are. Most of us need to do some inner work to dry out sufficiently in order to benefit from this second approach to self-inquiry. If you are a waterlogged sort like me, the observation that the ego is like all other concepts takes a while to assert itself. So, using the first method, you commit to examining your outer identifications one at a time. Each time one is released, corresponding small changes occur in the ego. Eventually, via the second method, you recognize that the ego itself is a concept, and the fundamental identification with being a separate self drops on its own. This is like our earlier metaphor of ornaments hanging on a Christmas tree. When you finally become disidentified, it's not because you've rearranged all of the ego ornaments; they fall by themselves because the tree has been cut down.

It is important to understand that the two methods usually work together; and for most people, they are not purely sequential. In practice, you will often find that after a period of meditating on the question "Who am I?" you bump up against more identifications and conditionings that block the recognition of the ego's disguises. So it's back to the mat for another round of process work. And to answer a question that you might be asking at this point: The process leading up to awakening takes as long as it takes.

In our history as a modern society, we generally have treated this type of work on the ego as a pursuit solely for personal growth. But this restriction is losing its grip. As globalization and enormous technological advances have been shrinking the size of our world community and exponentially increasing our immediate access to information, many of the boundaries that separated nations, fields of study and research, and even domains of consciousness have been eliminated. Accordingly, any sense that Awakened Leadership and personal inquiry are two separate phenomena is fading fast. It follows that much of what has been effective in individual process work is quickly migrating into the corporate world. Since being an awakened leader is the same as living any other aspect of your life within the awakened state, we can see that leadership development requires that you authentically engage in your own internal search.

The next three chapters, which touch on the topics of presence, service, and relationship, will help you to do that. Each of these chapters is a doorway, or a set of pointers, to a fundamental shift out of ego-identification. Read them with that in mind. You will know which doorways to pass through if you let your intuition draw you to them.

14 Walking on Sunshine

Some of the most startling shifts in my understanding have occurred on occasions when my children have shared their insights with me. One case in point is a conversation that I had with my son, Michael, when he was twelve years old. It went like this:

MIKE: I don't understand belief.

DAD: What don't you understand?

MIKE: Why do we need it?

DAD: Because it's part of life.

MIKE: But Dad, if we know something, we know it, right?

DAD: Yes.

MIKE: And if we don't know something, we don't know it, right?

DAD: Uh-huh.

MIKE: And if we're uncomfortable with not knowing, then we make something up and call it a belief, right?

DAD: Right.

MIKE: Well, why don't we just say what we know, not say what we don't know, and save ourselves the trouble of having to create belief?

In his youthful innocence, my son had stumbled on a startling fact: Most of the content in the human mind functions as a buffer to a large group of sensitive egos who simply can't tolerate not knowing. Michael had seen the truth that the emperor had no clothes on.

This perception gives rise to the further insight, mentioned in the previous chapter, that nothing is fixed or absolute. Why? Because any belief, absent direct knowledge, assumes the veracity of certain facts, some or many of which are unknown or unverifiable. This reduces belief to the category of fiction. Now most people bridle at the notion that all belief is a fiction. So they miss the good-news guarantee that any reality can be shifted. The invitation to awakening is actually an invitation to open to the deeper shifts that occur as the personal beliefs that hold our ego-based reality in place dissolve. As the identification with our beliefs—indeed, with the very belief in belief itself—begins to give way, the tension of trying to maintain control relaxes, and who we really are is realized and can be lived fully for the first time. It turns out that we are much more than what the ego offers on its menu of fixed beliefs and assumed knowledge.

So where do we start? The answer to that is beyond the realm of concept and the beginning of the trek into experience. In order to expand into that understanding, first we must give up our mindless worship of concept as though it were experience. Then, with the same immediacy that we know whether something we are eating is cold, hot, sweet, salty, or bitter, we can know where breakthroughs are possible. Yes, it is that direct. But how do we get access to that type of knowing?

In all of manifestation, the particulars that make up daily life are available to be extracted and then fixed into patterns that result in various forms of bondage. The more we become fixed, the more that everything that connects to us becomes fixed as well, and vice versa. This bondage will ultimately be recognized as an illusion, but until that time, any identified particular in our fixed constellation defines our felt experience of reality. As difficult as it is to distinguish the specific identifications that we hold, and then disidentify from them, at least we can sense that something exists beyond our fixation. This intuition, and our willingness to leave the land of fixedness, is our starting point.

I have used the awareness of fixed identification to create new stories and change the nature of my presence in any situation. This does not eliminate the need to do whatever is necessary to deliver on the value propositions that any of us has committed to and consistently provide high-quality responses. But the sense of presence creates for those we serve an umbrella that is much larger than our smaller selves; it situates all of us in the presence of Awakened Leadership. Haven't you felt that sense in those you consider effective leaders? What you are feeling is that umbrella of presence and your own expanded possibility.

Some of you may be familiar with the adventures of the redoubtable James T. Kirk, captain of the starship *Enterprise*. As a young cadet, Jim Kirk had to undergo a training exercise that was the dread of every man or woman who had a yen for the captain's chair. A crisis situation of epic proportions was programmed as a simulation into the ship's computer, and it was the responsibility of the trainee to "save" the *Enterprise* and her crew from utter disaster. This simulation was called the no-win scenario because there was actually no solution; the ship would blow up no matter what options were tried. But Kirk was the first cadet in the entire history of Starfleet Academy who did not fail the test. How did he do it? Realizing that there was no way out—given the parameters of the exercise—he found a way to reprogram the simulation. His explanation? "I don't believe in the no-win scenario."

His superior officers and the program simulators were so miffed at being outsmarted that they tried to discredit Kirk's success. They insisted that he had cheated, but in the end, they had to admit that he had gone so far beyond the rules that he could not be accused of breaking them. Our hero didn't let himself be conquered by the fixed idea that there was nothing he could do to save the ship. And his approach to the exercise went beyond even what we call thinking outside the box. It required a sense of possibility and presence that thumbed its nose at the common definition of problem solving. The point of the exercise had been to see how a would-be captain reacted when no more options were left in a disaster, but Kirk never let his actions be defined by the agendas of fixed identification.

This may lead you to believe that all of your actions are generated by a self that has control over its circumstances simply by dint of having superior intelligence, a strong will, or a passionate desire to succeed. Our sense of doership is so embedded in our belief system that we are sure it is real. But this viewpoint can lead to significant frustration. If we make a choice and things work out to our satisfaction, then we pat ourselves on the back. In contrast, when a chosen course of action doesn't take us where we plan to go, we delete the entire episode from our database so that it won't influence our future decisions or, even more important, disturb the piece of our self-identity that is linked to that decision. It's not difficult to see that when this system is in place, our ego keeps getting reinforced, whether the outcomes please us or not.

When I was growing up, our family lived approximately twenty miles from Disneyland. One of the rides, Autopia, has small cars that run on fixed tracks through some scenery and are equipped with a steering wheel that one can easily see is connected to no other part of the car. Whenever a child turns the wheel to the right and the car turns to the right, you can see a happy, smiling face. That same face displays puzzlement or distress as soon as that kid turns the wheel to the right but the car turns left.

If we can imagine these cars symbolizing who we think we are, and the drivers as the intellect that we believe controls our journey, an interesting observation can be made. How many times in your own life have you turned the wheel to the right, found yourself going in the direction you intended, and believed that you had conquered the world? Probably thousands. But what happens when you turn your wheel to the right and end up moving in the opposite direction? Most of us immediately assume that either there is something wrong with the car or we need to google a driving school and sign up for a remedial course.

Children can be too young to understand that the tracks running underneath their cars at Disneyland determine the course their car will take. We adults see what is going on there, but we do not recognize that forces much bigger than ourselves create the tracks in our own lives that lead to certain outcomes. The magic of transformation lies in recognizing that there are forces at play that must be invited into our awareness. Once our "as if" concept of life is expanded experientially to include these forces, we will live into life as though we were a Formula One race car driver. This expansion is the key to presence and will leverage whatever gift you carry that is currently unexpressed or undeveloped.

Early in my career, while I was being mentored by a consummate merger/acquisition expert, I was on one occasion having difficulty letting go of part of a deal that I was in the midst of negotiating. At one point in this difficult discussion, my mentor stopped me in midflight as I was recounting over and over the part of the deal I could not release.

MENTOR: Imagine that you are on the freeway on a busy day with a lot of traffic all around you. All of a sudden, a speeding car overtakes you and then cuts you off in an apparently unthinking manner. What would be your reaction?

ALAN: [*demonstrates the one-fingered salute with his right hand and leans on an imaginary horn with his left*]

MENTOR: I assume by your reaction that you believe that the driver who cut you off did it purposely and unjustly.

ALAN: You got that right.

MENTOR: Okay. Let's say that the next day, you hear that a neighbor of yours had to rush his injured four-year-old to the hospital in your neighborhood and you realize that he was the guy who had cut you off. What would your reaction be now?

ALAN: If I had known, of course I would have immediately slowed down and figured out a way to make sure that he got to the hospital as quickly as possible.

We can see that each of us carries default stories that come into play whenever anything arises that triggers us. And it is obvious that once any scenario is shifted through understanding, an entirely different course of action and outcome become possible. Though most people see this point, they don't think to put it into practice. I realized that not only could I begin to perceive from a different perspective the events that were occurring in my life, but I could also create new stories that would produce results that had formerly seemed unreachable. So I began to practice.

My growing ability to shift my stories in business situations started to produce breakthroughs. For example, I was once assigned to do extensive work with medical and pharmaceutical clients. The problem was that I had grown up believing that medical personnel were of a higher order than I was and that I didn't belong in their world. A helpful colleague, noticing my discomfort in that environment, asked me if I knew how to walk through the halls of my other clients as if I owned the place. The point was clear; I knew how easy it was to do this, and the difference it made in how I was treated. So why not give it a try the next time I had an appointment at the largest hospital in Newport Beach?

The offices I needed to access in the hospital were often in areas where public entry was prohibited. I had become accustomed to getting stopped at every single checkpoint and questioned about where I was going and why. On the first day of practicing my new walk of presence, I pretended that I owned the hospital and that all the doctors reported to me. I walked right through all the Checkpoint Charlies with nary a glance from the folks who were there to weed out those who clung most tightly to their fixed identities.

Many people have the idea that awakening empowers the ego to master its surroundings. But in fact, awakening eliminates the ego's job of personal doership. The resulting shift to holding space allows what is entirely new and unforeseen to arise, moment by moment. Then each action that you take is launched from an entirely different platform: Your thoughts and actions become creative responses to what is, rather than attempts to control it. Opportunities to problem solve become possibilities for outcomes that are natural extensions of the moment rather than egocentric responses. That shift creates a presence that can be felt by everyone in your world, and particularly by those you lead. Changing the sense of presence that we experience and exude to those around us is a doorway to the possibility of a new felt experience for all concerned.

Early in my career, while still under the wings of my CEO group, I had the opportunity to make a pitch to what would be the largest client I had ever acquired on my own. At the time, the firm I had founded was generating about $750,000 annually. The potential client—a large skateboard, snowboard, and apparel distributor in Orange County—was a conglomerate of seven companies that was exceeding $50 million in annual revenue, moving quickly to the $100 million mark. I had calculated that the revenue that our company would generate by acquiring this account would be approximately $1.4 million. If you do the math, you will see that this new job would bring in approximately twice my company's income, increasing it to three times its size. At first I felt intimidated by the prospect, but because I had taught myself that any sense of intimidation is caused by a story that I carry within myself—typically an unconscious one—I knew that this situation merely called for a story change.

And so I created a story that cast me as a powerful entrepreneur within an emerging company that all large businesses like this distributor's were fighting to have as a consultant. By then I had perfected my entrance into any situation by using my "hospital walk." This immediately reprogrammed the scenario into one in which a larger presence was at play: The potential clients, surmising that I could come up with the types of solutions arrived at only by consultants of the highest caliber, would sign on. So that's the energy I took into the meeting, and the distributor hired our company on the spot. Somewhat unprepared to make such a big leap, my partners initially went into shock, but they soon recovered and we were able to pull it off.

It might sound as though I am proposing that you exude more self-confidence and become a more expansive doer. This is one of the commonly held theses of the self-mastery approach to leadership that we have all seen before. *But presence is not a doing; it develops as an allowing of what is.* No force or doership is needed. The simple surrender to your own possibility of awakening will teach you how to hold presence. While that may still sound like doing, it is not. As I have continually emphasized, concepts cannot convey true experience, and words simply point you to a larger outcome.

The true test of one's capacity to shift stories is found in situations that arise unexpectedly and demand an immediate response. After a period of practicing in advance for upcoming challenges, I noticed that my awareness that the world is not fixed and absolute began to emerge automatically even when I was unprepared. I had picked up another large client that had been experiencing problems with their previous CPA. This company manufactured fine metal parts for the largest guitar maker in the United States. Their CPA had told my client that corporate tax returns had been prepared and filed every year for the past three years. The client had never asked for copies of the returns, trusting that the CPA had executed them on his behalf. The accountant was eventually arrested for tax-filing fraud and now sat languishing in a nearby jail. Naturally, the CEO was worried that his company might attract the attention of the IRS.

I took him on as a client, and we agreed that my firm would begin to service their account as well as bring anything from the past into compliance. Less than a week after our first meeting, while gazing out at palm trees from the expansive glass window in my Irvine office, I received an urgent call from my client:

> CEO: Am I glad you're in. I'm here in my office with a criminal investigator from the state of California. He's just told me that there are no tax returns on file for our company for the past three years. Not only that, there are no personal returns for me either. He is just about to cuff me and throw me in jail. Plus he says I'm a flight risk. I'm supposed to appear before a judge tomorrow, where the prosecutor is going to ask that I be held without bail. I asked him if I could call my new CPA, and he said he would be willing to speak with you.

I'd only had an initial meeting with this client, followed by a request for documents that had not yet been delivered. I didn't have even a piece of paper with meeting notes, much less a company file on them. But I knew enough about this entrepreneur that I considered him to be an honorable participant in my world. And I knew that when this sense was present, I could simply allow that to extend out into the space in which I now found myself with the investigator. No force was necessary; I just needed to hold the door for the larger possibility to make itself known. So the exchange with the agent went something like this:

ALAN: Good afternoon, sir. This is Alan Shelton speaking. Can I help clear up this misunderstanding?

INVESTIGATOR: Mr. Shelton, I have your client here, and he has not filed personal or company tax returns for the past three years. Since I am assuming he had taxable income, he will owe taxes, penalties, and interest. Moreover, he has significant assets that would allow him to leave the jurisdiction if he so chose. So I intend to read him his rights and place him in custody for the court to make a decision.

ALAN: I understand your caution, but I can assure you that it is unnecessary. I don't provide services for anyone who lacks integrity. Not only is my client not a flight risk, he is a hard-working, high-value leader in the corporate community. I can produce whatever documents and tax returns you need to back up my words. No problem. Just give me a reasonable amount of time.

[A lengthy pause]

INVESTIGATOR: Mr. Shelton, I've never felt so swayed in a conversation from a position that I previously held. In this case, I feel that I can give you a four-week period to produce information that proves your client's innocence. If you agree to that time window, I won't proceed with the arrest. I'm doing this solely on your word, and I hope I'm not making a mistake here.

You can imagine that this story and others like it made the rounds in Orange County business circles and accrued to the benefit of my company and the people who were working so hard to make it great. All of this became possible through the simple understanding that life as we know it is a construction of stories, most of which were created for the purpose of protecting us when we were children, but which can now be changed through simple awareness.

This awareness can extend to even the most cherished notions about business practices. CPAs occupy the most traditional and fixed segment of the financial services industry. For hundreds of years, they have done business in specific ways that have been considered unchangeable. But just as the underlying story of any given situation can shift, so can the fixed systems that have been inherited from centuries of practice.

As a young entrepreneur with client companies that were preparing to be sold or go public, I saw that many of my own industry's methods were unwieldy. For example, the custom in all CPA firms is to bill clients based on cost per hour, even for merger and acquisition consulting. Hours are meticulously tracked and a detailed bill is delivered to the client. Having taken on this fixed belief of hourly billing, I did what everyone else was doing. This approach, however, creates two problems: First, one has to spend an inordinate amount of time at all levels within a company to track and account for the time spent during each billing period. The second problem is that some engagements and services are of much greater value to the client than others, requiring highly developed skill sets not easily found. So an across-the-board hourly rate vastly undervalues a lot of the work that is being done. I recognized that if my firm could carry the story of its value to the market, we could do away with cumbersome timekeeping systems and bill much more in revenues.

Unfortunately, the old story of tracking and billing hours is such an embedded assumption within the minds of CPAs that it took me six months to convince every other member of my firm that it would be better to change our approach. The day finally came when everyone was on board. We were poised to become the first firm of our kind to assign a dollar value for what we delivered that was based on what we thought it was worth on the market. I asked them all to practice their "hospital walk" as we prepared to inform all of our clients about the new billing practices. It was worth the effort. This new measure changed the entire feel of how our company operated. Gone were the days of clients demanding justification for hours billed and complaining about rates that were too high. Every client now knew exactly how much would be billed and exactly what we would produce. Not only that—because the entire staff was much more relaxed, they were able to produce better results.

What I have just described may seem to simply be a shift from one powerful personal belief to another, requiring no fundamental change of consciousness. But the real issue is more foundational. For almost everyone, the condition of being trapped in our current ego state, with all of its outcroppings in the world, seems intractable. But this is not the case. Our experience of who we are is, in fact, malleable. It is only our incorrect internal assumptions that keep us lashed to the mast of our ship of identification. In our struggle to free ourselves from the suffering that this bondage causes, it is easy to find advice, methods, tools, and opportunities to improve the externals in our lives, in the hope that our suffering will cease, or at least that our conditions will improve to the point where we can distract ourselves from the pain. But this approach amounts to simply moving the game pieces in one's environment.

At the base of all human behavior is the default script that there is an "I" that has the power to make things happen. That script convinces us that replacing one practice with another is going to make a difference. What is missing is the recognition that this "I" who is supposedly making that difference is as contrived as any other belief, practice, or system that has been taken on, rejected, or changed. So the real magic lies in our ability to shift our personal identification altogether. As long as there is a belief that this "I" is the author of our own output, much of the energy that is available to us will be spent in trying to strategize the approach of that "I". However, when it is recognized that all of manifestation is interlinked and arises as one piece, this "I" is simply lived into each moment.

This recognition, as I have pointed out before, cannot remain conceptual; it must nest itself in experience. Nisargadatta Maharaj once said, "A prince that believes himself to be a beggar can be convinced conclusively in one way only: he must behave as a prince and see what happens. Behave as if what I say is true and judge by what actually happens."[1] It turns out that we create all of manifestation—that is, life as we see it—by extracting the pieces that we prefer and acting as if they were real. When this "as if" nature is recognized, it is possible to see that this "I" is the same as any other concept. Once that happens, all of the mental effort previously invested in manipulating this "I" throughout one's life—as though it were independent of everyone and everything else—is released. The magic of life can now unfold and lead you, the seeker, to your unknown spiritual destination.

When I discuss such a radically new way of being, perceiving, and acting in the world, I notice that most people experience consistent and ongoing resistance, if not outright fear. The desire to engage me in some form of argumentation or debate generally follows. I often advise those who protest to consider any new approach that I am suggesting as though it were a pair of Levis. You currently are wearing an old, crusty pair, and you hardly know that you have them on. So you can simply take them off, put them on the hook, and try the new pair on. If it turns out that you don't like the new ones, the old ones are always available to put on again. This will make the entire process feel much lighter. It is much easier to change your tightly held concepts when you see that you have nothing to lose. They will wait for you patiently and will gladly reunite with you at any time.

Without a doubt, you can be thankful for the more or less safe ride that your familiar, beloved ego has given you thus far. But this doesn't mean that you have to spend the rest of your life at the ego's mercy and under its domination. Presence is already there and waiting, for it is your own expanded self. All that needs to happen in order to experience that bigger space is to release your attachments to what you think is inevitably real, unchangeably true, and eternally fixed. Nothing given up is lost. This makes the leadership experience a no-lose proposition.

With this recognition, you realize that your own awakening and the Awakened Leadership that springs from it are one and the same, because business stories and personal stories both live in a possibility of expansion into the larger presence that is you.

All of manifestation is available and held in presence. It is into that no-place that we find ourselves—every one of us—headed.

15 Just Say Yes

In our travels along the ego's path, we have seen that the fixed sense of "I" results in a felt sense of bondage. When we are in this state, our behavior is reactive and aimed at keeping our child-self safe—and, if we can manage, happy. At our last stop, we learned that, in contrast to the ego, our sense of presence is not fixed and can be expanded to include and resonate with our entire environment. When we are in this flexible mode, our behavior becomes creative. Instead of being locked into self-referential, predictable, reactive responses, our actions are now attuned to a bigger picture composed of infinite possibilities that invite our natural capacities to express themselves.

When I first stumbled into the world of being a seeker, I began to look for those possibilities. My life evolved into a combination of finding these wherever I could while at the same time continuing to encounter all the places where I was still identified. This divided my behavioral experience into two distinct parts: Whenever I located an opportunity to creatively expand, no sense of bondage was present. But when an unresolved identification triggered a reactive response in me, I became straightjacketed in a boundaried, separated "I". One facet of this reactive state was the tendency to label others' traits as negative. To my mind, everyone else's irritating habits and personality characteristics were the cause of my reactive judgments. Whenever I was uncomfortable, afraid, or insecure, I could take emotional refuge in my projections onto others. This thought pattern, a practiced repetition that I had learned as a child, experientially confirmed my ego-definition again and again. It was only when I began to accept my own negative traits that I could see that there was a way out of this repetitive two-step.

In the world of models, this process is known as reclaiming the shadow or as the integrative stage of maturation. These terms, however, don't quite capture the nature of the transformation that was occurring. For I had come to recognize that epiphanies surface on the seeker's path independent of the locus of their arising. For me, this meant that India-esoteric Alan, California-corporate Alan, and husband-and-father Alan were simply different soundtracks that were being played on the single stage called life. The changing costumes of the actors that entered and exited stage right and left at various times could not hide this fact. And so it could be seen that all of life can be embraced simultaneously. At that point, it was no longer necessary to keep my radar constantly tuned to potential transformational opportunities; now every event qualified. This was a significant shift from decades of ferreting out selected experiences within which to create, a method that excluded all the other experiences that did not make the cut.

Now I could seal that experiential divide by seeing every event not only as an opportunity to express my creative potential, but also as a way to serve others. As I did this, my experience of other people expanded beyond a rigid positive/negative polarization, and the self-referential misery of blame and victimhood continued to disappear. I knew that service needed to become my new mantra. The more I understood my actions to be expressions of the desire to serve, the clearer the calling would come into focus.

After my son was living with us for a while, and the euphoria of his presence wore off, I realized that being a full-time father again meant that interests higher than my own needed to be served. A perceptive judge had confirmed that it was in Michael's best interests to stay with me, but only as long as my son performed well scholastically and in his other activities. In a page torn from the story of the red hatchet, Michael didn't leave things to chance. He went for it with the same determination as the boy who, many years before, had set out in the rain every day to sell his boxes of chocolate. Michael went from a sixth grade of C's and D's to a seventh grade of straight-A honors. In fact, he received an award for being the best seventh grade student in the whole city.

My son had more than achieved his goal, but we knew that he needed to develop even more disciplined study habits in order to continue his education. In that spirit, together we made the decision to find a prep school where he could polish these skills. In 1999, tuition for such schools typically ran in excess of thirty thousand dollars a year, and the one we chose was no exception. So it was no surprise that when I asked if my ex-wife was willing to chip in for the tuition, the answer was a firm no. Perhaps most people in my position would have engaged in a blame game, citing irrefutable proof that the ex was being unreasonable, selfish, uncaring, spiteful, or simply unaware. My friends and loved ones, and even my children, could find no way to see this situation other than through the lens of separation. But amidst a sea wave of suggested tactical responses, such as "Find a way to get even" or "Make her feel guilty," a different course opened up as soon as I saw that the situation was not really about me.

Life had chosen me to play the role of father and leader of our ragtag little pack and, when I looked forward rather than backward, the point became obvious: My son needed to go to that school in order for his life to move ahead, and I simply had to find a way to make that happen. And so, despite occasional lapses, I shifted to the place of being in service to my son. Once I arrived there, nothing could interfere with the leadership role that I had gladly taken on. This may sound like giving Alan a pat on the back, but the reality of the situation is that it was only from beyond the small-Alan ego that decisions like these could emerge. Saying no, criticizing and blaming, feeling superior, are all easy to do from the ego-self position. The former Alan would have never made the decisions I did; he would have been more interested in being right and admired, blasting through obstacles with his superior strength and stamina. Turning a no into a yes, shifting resistance to apparent barriers into nonresistance, and simply moving with what the situation presented required an expanded sense of service to be in place.

Life has a funny way of repeating circumstances again and again, providing wonderful opportunities to gauge the difference in our responses over time. Four years later, after graduating from prep school, my son was accepted to the University of Arizona. Once again, Debbie refused to participate in his financial support. This time, I noticed that the chorus criticizing my ex-wife—and me for my refusal to "fight for what was right"—had quieted down dramatically. So, two years later, when my daughter was accepted to the University of Southern California, I readied myself to face the double-barreled shotgun of both kids' college expenses. My ex-wife must have known that I would opt for the same course that I had previously chosen. I may never know the reason why, but she contacted me to offer some support. We negotiated an agreement for my daughter and, not only that—Debbie even volunteered to begin sending my son spending money.

I'm not sure that I can claim to be the cause of my ex-wife changing her course. I do know that I was only too happy to accept the help that was offered toward the goal that Existence had called me to execute. And that when I embraced all of the educational opportunities for my children as though I were a leader in charge of completing a mission, keeping my focus on the initiatives at hand, the sharp differences that defined that battle line between Debbie and myself disappeared.

This story may sound like an old divorced guy getting in a cheap shot. But the fact is that the connection with my ex-wife held the loudest "No!" of any relationship I had at that time. I felt that if I could turn even that situation around with my yes, then this new approach would have real legs in my life. I have felt no ill will toward Debbie since then; in fact I'm impressed by her expanded responses to our children. Did she and I pass through a time of fixed and immature behavior to arrive where we are today? Yes, we did. But in the spirit of the service that we both ultimately provided on our children's behalf, I am thankful for how it all turned out.

Through this experience, I came to see that the path to awakening is full of opportunities to turn every no born of resistance or stubbornness into a yes. What I discovered is that each time I moved into that place, everybody concerned seemed to benefit in some way. This is because a field gets created in which the yes of even one person within a given situation or dynamic inspires a natural movement of everyone else toward expanded action. This expansion results in decisions that fit themselves into the flow of life, even if they appear to be messy, inconvenient, illogical, or unfair. Within that field, ego boundaries dissolve and outcomes emerge gracefully. In this sense, service is not the outcome of abstract moral ideals; *it is simply the recognition of how the nonegoic self functions.*

This principle of service went beyond laying down my sword on the battlefield of entrenched positions and extended into the already flourishing relationship with my wife, Justine. For years after we married, Justine willingly shouldered the role of support person in all aspects of our life. She accepted the tough job of managing two children during the most difficult years of their lives. At the same time, she was providing all the administrative support to my burgeoning practice. When my children began their college careers, Justine began to feel the urge to express her own creativity and interests. She had become an ardent practitioner of yoga, and her early experiences with horses made it obvious that she had a healer's touch. Just as the earnings based on my market value in the executive world had been able to serve my kids' educational needs, they could now serve my wife.

So Justine embarked on a training course that developed her into an acclaimed yoga therapist and alternative healer. To this day, she treats patients with cancer, diabetes, PTSD, or any other condition that requires her love. Every night, she comes home and recounts the stories of her interactions with the people whom she serves. She always starts off by telling me their names and, of course, I can't keep most of them straight. But I don't see these people as merely her clients; they are part of our family. When she needs to do something on their behalf, especially when it doesn't fit particularly well in our schedule, I never think in terms of "How is this going to work for me?" but rather "What does this beloved within our family need and how can we provide that?" Viewed through the typical lens of separation, it looks as though my consulting practice provides the main financial support for my wife's activities. Our felt experience is that we both do what we love, and people are healed and served as a result. Again, there is no line of demarcation.

The melting of the illusory division called "Those are your goals and interests, and these are mine" and the accompanying sense of being part of a larger family spilled over into my embrace of service in the business world. It was obvious that my ability to produce maximum income lay in the particular skill set for which the market would consistently pay the highest amounts. But although my career had yielded a very good living, it did not include the type of service that now would become a natural extension of my seeker's life. When I stepped off the ledge and plummeted into the seeker's world, a higher priority than my own bottom line in dollars and cents took hold, and the essence of what service truly is began to express itself in corporate leadership.

Fortunately, I had maintained my connections with the world of CEOs and was ideally qualified and prepared to lead companies. So I began to accept two- and three-year CEO assignments. These companies needed intense management help—now. For early-stage opportunities, the time fuse to extinction is always short; the same is true for troubled companies looking for an exit. It now was up to me to lead my companies through these turbulent passages.

The first opportunity arose when I was asked to take over the investment arm of a growing restaurant chain. In the late nineties, healthy Mexican food became very popular with restaurant goers in Southern California. I had been introduced by one of my clients to a restaurant operator who managed a chain called Chico's Tecate Grill. My client was interested in the investment opportunity but concerned about the questionable growth velocity of the company. The chain was successful in all of its locations due to its tasty recipes and use of healthy ingredients, and it had done well for all the franchisees. However, there were too few restaurants and insufficient capital to produce a growth rate that would guarantee the success of the parent company, the franchisor. My client and I decided to form an investment company that would partner with the restaurant company; this model had been used extensively and successfully by several of the larger restaurant companies in the United States.

The new investment arm faltered right out of the gate. It had been a good idea in theory, but the organization needed to be led forward from its original vision. I was called in by my client to manage the company— if I thought it could succeed. I took the challenge. Over a period of two years, the investment company funded eighteen new restaurants in the chain, and I had my first opportunity as a CEO to lead from a place of all-embracing service. My own yes snowballed into an entire company saying yes. It wasn't a perfect flow, but this approach held a place for all the team members to stand in their own personal process. Awareness became a group holding, and the bumpy ride was a perfect vehicle for our corporate tour.

You might prefer to hear that this story had a successful outcome in the world's terms. But in this case, while the service response was in perfect, symphonic pitch, the company did not make it. The external factors were too much to overcome. Do I consider this a wasted part of my career? No. Just as our held boundaries between the corporate and personal worlds are simply concepts, so is the difference between success and failure. It was on the stage of failure that the script of awakening placed the character called Alan at that time. I was as much a leader there as I had been when people were applauding and throwing flowers on the stage after a successful run. Today, when I coach a CEO of a company, I do not care if the ship she captains is listing. I have walked on that deck before, and awakening holds no regard for the level of deferred maintenance of the craft you guide.

The next time I was tapped for a CEO role, the circumstances were even more challenging. In early 2003, I was contacted by a group of investors who had funded a large flower-distribution company in

Miami. Bloss was founded, together with its original investment group, by a youthful, energetic management team. These young guys were the best and brightest in other companies in the flower business and were well acquainted with many growers in Colombia and Ecuador. Because of these relationships, and their reputation as young bucks in the industry, the growers had gladly advanced floral product. However, the typical rookie mistake was made of building a company for a future that had yet to arrive. Much of the invested capital had been squandered on unnecessary facilities and management. The monthly income flow was not sufficient to pay their investors and suppliers, who were running out of patience. The good news was that the company had loyal customers and the prospect of adding more.

I was asked to analyze the company's prospects. If I found that the positive outweighed the negative, then an exit plan could be created, rather than just allowing the company to implode. I did my due diligence and concluded that there was a significant upside to attempting a resurrection of this company—but also a substantial risk. The investors asked me to consider a two-year CEO contract after which they would sell the company. This was going to be a real test of a service notion of leadership.

The young management team was not enamored of the idea of selling the company in such a short time frame. But their weak financial position left them no choice except to stay with it in order to realize any profit at all. The suppliers had advanced more than three million dollars of product and were not in a trusting or generous mood. These two factors combined to decrease the level of service, and customers were beginning to notice. Even in this uneasy atmosphere, I could see that, given the correct financial structure, we could meet the goals of the investors and benefit the management team as well. We would also be able to pay back all of the suppliers for their valuable product.

The question in my mind was whether all of these parties with their different self-interests could stay connected through sharing the ultimate goal of saving the company. Was it possible to consistently have them keep this outcome in mind and embrace it experientially while placing their opinions, immediate needs, and doubts on hold? I didn't know. But from a deeper level than my analyses of problems and potentials, the yes response to the opportunity emerged. Leadership was needed, and my yes started the clock.

The first step was to meet all of the suppliers. Numbering some sixty-five in total, they were located within reach of three cities: Quito in Ecuador, and Bogota and Medellin in Colombia. With the CFO and COO of Bloss, I met with every one of them in the course of five days. The arrangement I proposed wouldn't warm the heart of a typical supplier. I could offer them only a small fraction of the balance owed, while asking them to hold off for ninety days for the next payment, plus send new product in the meantime. I knew that the only way they would buy this plan was if it seemed possible for the company to make it. And so I told them this story:

> A large caravan of bedouins with pack animals carrying heavy supplies was winding its way up a circular path to the top of a mountain. The path was only about six feet wide, and the caravan was easily five hundred yards in length. As the path neared the summit, a large rock blocking the entire path came into view. Of course, the caravan had to stop.
>
> When such things happen, the natives at the back get restless, especially because they can't see what has brought everything to a halt. What these men *could* see was the valley several thousand feet below. Nervous, some of them fell to fighting among themselves. Finally, one of the drivers ran to the front and asked the caravan leader, "What should I do? They're fighting back there!" In response, the leader said, "Bring them up here and show them the rock."

If you want someone to understand a problem, you need to show them the rock; the issue at hand has to be accessible and clearly visible. Doing that was my job. I imagine that, to this day, a number of those suppliers chuckle at the memory of an animated gringo translating an old Sufi caravan story into Spanish in order to convince them that the company could succeed. I don't know whether it was the humor or my sincerity that convinced them, but all sixty-five agreed to continue. When the management team and the investors were briefed on what had happened, they all asked me to tell them that Sufi story. And they too became part of the little caravan that now included everyone involved in making our new plan work.

Some two years later, we were able to sell off all the company's assets. Part of my role was to keep the sense of mission intact and periodically pull out of the ditch those who lost touch with it. My success at keeping everyone connected to our service objective was intermittent. The experience was tough. But I knew that I was where I needed to be. Life had lived me into this herky-jerky version of service. The result could have been judged as a win, a loss, or a draw. But the yes to service superseded the bottom line.

Companies can ascend, falter, limp along, recover, succeed, fail. The call to service is the same at any point. It was now obvious that my ego was no longer in charge of selecting where my service would take place, for my engagement was now coming from a much bigger place. The space of yes, as a response to what I intuitively sensed was arising for me to participate in, was that place.

The importance of understanding service as the on-the-ground experience of integration, or reclaiming the shadow, is monumental. On paper, "integration" and "reclamation" sound like lofty concepts. These words fit nicely into squares and circles connected by neatly drawn lines. But one who has experienced full immersion into service understands that life doesn't work that way. One day, you and your management team are at a particular place, and the awareness needed to make a course correction points in a certain direction. The following day, the necessary correction might be in exactly the opposite direction. Life does not happen in a smooth curve that starts with a vision and ends in euphoria. Events, as they occur in any experience of manifestation, have a beginning, middle, and ending, which are all characterized by complications, uncertainties, and wild cards.

We resist this fact because we have not yet learned that we don't need to know outcomes in advance, and that only in not knowing can we truly be in the flow of life. Most of us are familiar with plane travel, so we have been exposed to the speech about putting on oxygen masks in case of an unknown turbulence: First we do our own and then we help the kids. The ego wants to know in advance what to do in case it encounters turbulence. So we desperately seek instructions and advice as though our life depended on it. *Awakened Leadership is the recognition that the only stable thread that weaves itself through your experience and that of the people you lead is the internal peace that you contribute to the fray.* This sense of peace is not your possession. However, you are the one who has the open aperture of awareness that it is always accessible. In essence, you lend the experience of peace to everyone else by holding space. In this way, everyone moves into peace and has an experience of what has always been their natural birthright.

No matter where you are on the arc of experience, you are here and now. And at every point of here and now, you are faced with the option of saying yes or saying no. You may have arrived at this point with the questions, How can I tell where my yes or my no is coming from? What is the felt experience that confirms that my assent to a certain course of action is in the flow? There is a difference between an authentic yes and a contrived one—that is, a yes based on obligation, fear, reaction, or egoic striving. In order to understand that difference, we need to remember that the ego, as we have discussed before, fills its space with concentrated content. This content, called belief, crowds out the natural space of the unknown from which creative outcomes emerge. Recognize that it is from our position within the web of belief that we are accustomed to asking our questions and taking a certain path. But a true yes arises out of the unknown essence of our being, a space that opens only when Belief Central closes its doors. Then our felt experience is that we are in and part of the flow, and that this flow embraces and includes us plus everything and everyone else.

In that experience, "looking out for number one" has no meaning. There is no conflict between taking care of ourselves and helping others. We are all number one. In fact, even the question of what to choose doesn't arise. We appear to be making choices, but we are simply being lived into the unknown frontier of authenticity. It is to that frontier that the best leaders lead their troops. Through recognizing their own optimal position in any given moment, they know when they need to be out in front. Great leaders don't force themselves into that position; they let themselves be drawn there, and naturally create the atmosphere in which every other person on the team knows where he or she needs to be in order to meet the common objectives of the whole enterprise.

Throughout my time in the corporate world, and on the seeker's path, I have consumed inordinate amounts of observations, advice, and instructions. Leadership is a topic that is rife with all of these things. Ultimately, the question is not whether you have read and cognized all of these concepts. The question is whether the attributes of leadership, which are the same as those of seeking, live in you. This is especially true when one arrives at the opportunity to be in service, which is to say, to act outside the definition of ego. And while it is possible to describe the continuum of the reactive, creative, and integrated stages of human development, what matters is whether and how the attributes of Awakened Leadership show up in the experience of your life.

When my first master, Osho, advised us to "get experience," he was building the bridge to the other shore, which lies opposite our misinformed or incomplete concept of what integration is. It is only there that we find real experience in all of its unpredictable manifestations. The stage of integration lives in the experiential domain, not the theoretical; it therefore does not contain objects with conceptual definitions. You and everyone around you simply arise in the same flow and arrive at the same destination, which is here and now.

16 The Dangling Conversation

To make any headway in a discussion about relationships, some understanding of the composition of the world we live in is necessary. We find ourselves in manifestation, which is commonly referred to as duality. Duality is simply the notion that one thing can be identified because of its contradistinction with something else. This contrast is a matter of difference. Usually, the things that are diametrically opposite to each other are called complementaries. Because of the nature of duality, contrasting phenomena can be recognized separately but always arise together. If you recall the ancient Chinese symbol representing yin and yang, you will notice that the two complementary forms it contains occupy the space inside a complete circle. This is much like the world we live in, which is filled with diametric opposites that are wrapped together within one globe.

At the same time, there is no denying that these divergent energies move toward one another such that they appear together. For instance, as much as humans seek to distance themselves from death, it still appears as often as life. So we can say that the nature of duality is exactly this: the absolute necessity of there being two opposite but complementary energies within the same atmosphere, creating one whole.

As we have seen, the basic problem with humans is that they believe that they are entities with the ability to author their own script in life. This sense of being the doer often includes the apparent choosing of options that attempt to split the complementaries, which results in calamity. This is to engage in what we call dualism, as opposed to the acceptance of the obvious differences among the phenomena arising from duality. That is to say, humans have the annoying habit of picking one complementary aspect and enshrining it while attempting to ignore or destroy its unwanted opposite. This is much like deciding that all the quarters in your pocket should only have heads; you simply pretend that the tails side doesn't exist, despite what your eyes are telling you.

Interestingly enough, the ego is constructed in exactly the same way: It is the selection and amalgamation of the side we prefer of all of the coins in our collection. Instead of recognizing complementary opposites as being united, we set one side of the coin against its conjoined twin. Thus the ego spends its life busily engaged in a continuous shuffle of embracing the aspects of ourselves that we prefer, and denying—up to and beyond the point of unconsciousness—those we do not. In this exhausting battle for ego dominance, any awareness of the truth of our oneness is suppressed.

Is there a way out? Of course there is! Within the frustration of a lifetime of raging polarities, the map of maturation indicates a passage called the reclaiming of the shadow self. Reclaiming the shadow means welcoming back all the parts of ourselves that we have rejected in an effort to ensure that our disowned aspects will never make an appearance. Until the ego tension of constant surveillance is completely eliminated, it creates turbulence not only in our own minds and hearts, but also in all our relationships.

You see, there is one major problem with picking one complementary over another. These different energies have but one thing on their minds. Like hormone-drunk teenagers, they will stop at nothing to be together. It is irrelevant that the human mind has decided that they are separable. Some years ago, I was exposed to the now famous book *Men Are from Mars, Women Are from Venus* by John Gray. I was struck by the imagery of the two sexes being from entirely different planets with completely different orbits, yet part of the same universe. One thing I noticed was the inhabitants of Venus like to form themselves in groups and hold seemingly never-ending conversations about the problems in their lives. This evidently makes them feel better and more supported, and the discussions bring in more points of view, which can only help in sorting out ongoing perplexing situations. When I attempted anything of the sort with my fellow Martians, they would scatter as if I had thrown a live hand grenade into their midst. So my conclusion was that Mars is a lonely place. But that line of thought is a sample of the silliness of dualism. Despite protests to the contrary, there is no such place— because men and women stop at nothing to live on the same planet.

In previous chapters, we have discussed at length how our ego identification glues us to our own narrow perception, creating bondage and suffering. Nowhere is this more evident than in the confusing but irresistible activity of connecting with other human beings. Even more than to money and objects that have value, our mind assigns to our relationships a solidity that places them on the main stage of the three-ring circus that we call life. Relationships, especially those with the most marked polarities, generate the most powerful bonds. And it is axiomatic that wherever the glue is strongest, the misery index follows suit.

The nature of my relationships is no different. In this chapter, I concentrate on a few that are etched on the walls of my personal Grand Canyon. The value of understanding how one can accept and surrender to the world of opposites is much more easily perceived when those opposites are in such high contrast. It doesn't mean that those relationships are easier to navigate; they are just easier to see and thus to learn from. Perhaps the stories on this topic are more entertaining than some of the others in this book, but they are based on exactly the same ego mechanics that we have been exploring. And so we enter into the universe that I have labeled "the frustration of complementaries." Avoid the meteors on the right and the planets on the left, and we will see that this universe could be no different than it is.

The natural arc of ego development can be most easily seen in the various relationships of any individual. Keeping the ego defined is the highest priority within any relationship, so it is worthwhile to understand how this comes about. The early stages of the human journey begin with an infant establishing a sense of self-definition inherited from those who serve up dollops of conditioning. For a little boy, the major relationship most often is with his mother. Perhaps because my mother gave birth to me when she was only seventeen, her highest priority was for both of us to be safe in the world. And since she immediately named me after the major heartthrob of that time, Alan Ladd, I carried a self-definition that was based in large measure on her relating to me more as a companion than as her son. It is true that I was very close to my grandfather during that time, but it was my mother and I who lived in that apartment above the garage at his house—just the two of us—for my first few years.

My biological father, whom I never met, was apparently a larger-than-life character and was the love of my mother's life. It was a huge blow when, due to my grandmother's challenge of this man to step up to the plate and marry her daughter, he chose to exit a budding future with my mother and me. It was Mom who fed me, bathed me, and included me in the battle of the single unwed mother in 1950s America.

Due to a variety of painful factors, my mother's highly ambitious nature was not allowed to fully express itself. My strongest psychological memory of my mother is that she lived in the constant frustration of not being able to access her own potential. In her vicarious reach toward her dreams, she focused her attention on her children, especially on me as the eldest. My stepfather always seemed to be disgruntled that he could never meet my mother's expectations of him. From what I could tell, the reverse was also the case. So my early development had its foundation on the need to perform at a level that would please my mom and assist her in keeping us both feeling secure. In all of the personality evaluations that I have taken throughout my corporate and spiritual lives, one predominant theme has always emerged: The survival of Alan would depend on performing at a high level in order to receive the feedback from his environment that he was indeed safe. So, hands down, performance became the basic building block of my life.

Thus it is no surprise that the relationships that dot the path called Alan's life have performance as their chief feature. My very first girlfriend in high school, Sandie, was by all accounts the best student in town. During the prior year, in ninth grade, I had decided to see what it was like to relieve myself of getting good grades. I had been eminently successful in obtaining a D average. But when I met Sandie in the beginning of my sophomore year, something deep down called on me to perform at the highest possible level. That is to say, in this relationship, the space that my ego had occupied all alone now contained a girl whom I wanted not only to impress but also outdo. The boy who was able to sell more chocolates than any other Scout revved up his engines and went back into action. I got straight A's for the rest of my high school career. My teachers could just as well have drawn little red hatchets on my report cards for the next three years. In retrospect, it is obvious that the person I thought I was felt that he had no other choice except to excel by dominating in this area of performance. It was the only use for himself that he could intuit at that young age.

This pattern continued as I entered my early twenties. If you remember, upon leaving my two-year mission in Peru, I was advised to find an upstanding Mormon girl to become my wife for time and all eternity, which I did a couple of months later back at BYU. As it is in many youthful relationships, the energy between us started out light and wonderful and sexually charged. However, the Mormon Church, like most institutions, is a standard bearer for the concept that human-made rules control the energy of existence. Having been a Mormon bishop myself, I was expected to be not only a follower but also a guardian of those rules. But no matter how much ego control I tried to exert, and no matter how well trained my fiancée was in obedience to the Church, we "fell into sin." We were therefore required to make our confessions before a bishop and then spend a year in a sexless engagement to prove that we were worthy to get married in the Temple.

Debbie and I were able to accomplish that task, but the result was that much of the wonderful new energy that we shared when we first met drained away. Nonetheless, we did serve one another's definition of a perfect couple composed of a high-level-performance husband and a beautiful and also high-performing wife, plus we had our two beautiful children to show for our union. But when I became motivated to look more deeply into what life was offering me, it became apparent that our formulaic relationship would not withstand any kind of activity beyond the definitions we had mutually imposed upon our relationship. As soon as I began to open to a different future from what Debbie and I initially envisioned for our marriage, my own polarities began to shift. From that point on, my definitions of who I was started to lose their grip.

A second, much briefer, marriage was to follow. Unlike Debbie, my second wife had some authentic capacity for intimacy, but I unconsciously chose, once again, a woman whose traditional mindset and social rigidity could not support a new seeker. If I had continued to provide cars, houses, country club memberships, and credit cards, I suppose it could have worked. On second thought, cancel that—it just wasn't to be. I had solved one piece of the puzzle of relationship, but the rest was left scattered around the table.

My relationship life evolved into its second stage around the time I arrived in India for the first time, in 1991. At the ashram, it was commonly held that sexual energy is something that needs to be fully lived. Conditioning, on the other hand, attempts to control that energy and direct it into acceptable channels. In following a particular method and set of directives that is not actually the mind's job to select, the resulting out-of-balance condition of repression makes itself felt with a vengeance, inhibiting the possibility of awareness. It was with this new understanding that I began to engage in a variety of relationships with beginnings, middles, and endings all intertwining. In an atmosphere soaked in meditation and a collective commitment to increasing one's awareness, I began to simply watch what arose, sometimes allowing my life to be lived by energies larger than myself.

Even though it sounds as though relationships in an environment much more open than the one I came from would be ideal for me, this was not the case. You must remember that the participants in the ashram experience were living somewhere between their own fixed conditioning and the new life that they sought. So the beauty of connecting freely was sometimes marred by heavy pieces of our old conditioning being dragged through the beautifully manicured gardens of Zen perfection. Nonetheless, I could feel the definition that had been so tightly governing my engagement in relationship beginning to lose its tension. The women who entered into my life were different than those I had been with before. No longer was I attracting power brokers and competitors. For the first time, I found some room inside my connections with women to experience the kind of sensitivity, presence, and creativity that I'd never had the opportunity to blend with before.

It can be seen clearly that for the majority of my life, the hallmark of my intimate relationships was the attempt to be something for others that fulfilled my own self-definition and met some sense of theirs. This pattern begins in childhood, when one is struggling to define oneself in the world. As we grow up, we begin to feel more secure in our ability to deliver that self-definition, and we become clued in to the fact that we are also being asked to take in the definitions of other persons as they present theirs. So, because every individual believes that he or she is a solid, discrete entity, relationships become an exercise in doing two things at once. The first is this defining of ourselves for the other person.

Over the years, I have taken it upon myself to eavesdrop on random conversations as I sit in restaurants, coffee shops, and the like. This is a very entertaining thing to do. If you try it, you will be surprised to notice that probably eighty percent of all the exchanges consist of people describing to one another who they are. This behavior is probably more marked in people who are just getting to know one another: "I am very dependable" . . . "My friends say that I am very creative" . . . "In such-and-such situation, I would be like this" and so on.

While this delivery is being executed, a second function is simultaneously occurring—taking in the definition of the other person, who is as steadfastly dedicated to his task as you are to yours. When all this describing is done, we then determine if we have a mutually acceptable, viable option for pursuing a relationship. Of course, all of this description is aimed at establishing the value of the space that one occupies. For instance, I am a performer, so my "elevator speech" overflows with all of my performer qualities.

This behavior doesn't stop when you've established a bond with someone; it continues throughout the course of the relationship. The reality is that you can never escape how someone else defines you in his mind. As each of you changes over time, it becomes necessary to adjust how you describe yourselves. So the ego spends an astonishing amount of energy creating, revising, and re-revising its Facebook page and then delivering it so that someone else can know who you are. When you aren't being seen in the way that your ego demands, you intuitively know it, and that's when the trouble begins. If your complementary loses his or her fix on you, one or both partners have to add, subtract, or alter parts of their definition in order to keep the equation in balance. If the two of you cannot at least appear to remain sufficiently compatible, you move out of agreement and into conflict.

So we spend our relationship life climbing a slippery slope, only to fall to the bottom every time our mutually held self-definitions move out of sync; and if significant rifts are not bridged, the relationship breaks apart. In this process, we forget that the ego's demands that our definitions remain fixed and safe create an impossible condition. All coins do indeed have a tails side.

One of my favorite concepts, which I have lifted guiltlessly from the Buddha himself, is—and I paraphrase—all misery is rooted in our inability to accept what is. The dance of relationship merely reflects how Buddha saw the torturous life of a seeker: as another exercise in dealing with the ego's rejection of what exists in the moment. My version of his observation is: *Defining yourself as a separate ego-entity, which cannot help but resist what is, will cause your suffering.* But when it is seen that this ego is merely a part of everything that is arising, then the surrender to what is becomes included in that insight. Buddha would call this liberation.

As this awareness expands in you, you begin to lose the identification with the ego. The glue loosens. You are no longer bounded by the "little you," because you see yourself as one with all that is. Yes, you continue to act, but not with the identified fervor of someone who has to keep his ego defined, acknowledged, ratified, approved, or admired. So your actions happen but are not driven or forced. You feel that you are in the flow.

From this awakened perspective, relationships can arise as they normally do, but tightly held definitions can now unwind, and one is much more at ease with the stark differences that relationships reflect. Egos no longer clamor to dominate or to fill the entirety of the relationship space. There is no longer any need to construct a self that is composed of what we consider to be desirable characteristics while disowning everything that we deem unacceptable or unappealing. Rather, it is recognized that one's self and the self of the other, which include the full range of characteristics in both, simply arise, as everything else does.

At that point, the shadow elements of the personality have been reclaimed, and a deep relaxation sets in. This leads to an expanded, directly felt experience of one's own being and of awakening itself. Instead of continuing in its belief that it is a separate ego that needs to establish its definition for others, the body-mind comes to recognize that it can simply surrender into whatever is. There is no longer an individual ego hard at work making stressful efforts to define itself and accomplish its own objectives. From that time forward, everything in one's experience is understood from a completely new vantage point.

At this stage, relationship can now act as a device for witnessing. The hallmark of a relationship of this nature is a distinct lack of turbulence. Differences, when witnessed, are held as simply what's so; thus they don't compete. You find that you no longer need to convince the other person of anything and, in fact, there is no one left to do the convincing. Short of this realization, the tempestuous aspect of relationships continues to be a felt experience that cannot be denied. So, whether in a personal or leadership context, the seas of relationship froth and brew. But the maturation process, which includes the reclamation of the rejected parts of our being, eventually enlarges our felt sense of all manifestation, bringing the peace that seekers seek and leaders lead from.

The expanded experience described above is a form of holding space. We are able to be that peace-filled space for another person, which in some way signals to them that they are safe and can open up to that peace for themselves. In that sense, interestingly enough, all coaching is an exercise of the device that we call relationship. If a coach can simply hold space, rather than clinging to and imposing definitions, then issues that appear impossible to solve no longer derail coaching outcomes. The coaching process will hold all of the seeming disparities while the solution makes itself known.

I think that the terms "identification" and "holding space" can be brought into sharper focus in our understanding by revisiting our little story of the emperor's new clothes. Most people spend their entire life engaged in describing and debating about the wardrobe of the royal family, thereby confirming—to themselves and anyone who will listen—their assumption that the clothes are there in the first place. This is the approach of those who traffic in the fixed belief of being an ego. For when it is seen that the clothes really don't exist, one is left to simply watch the gawkers on the parade route describe a nude man as though he were king.

17 Everybody Into the Pool!

The seeker's path to freedom from the felt bondage of the ego has been described in all great mystical traditions down the centuries. Our rich human history of the search for truth has birthed many contemplative practices, such as meditation, prayer, and yoga. Whatever forms the search has taken, however, the legacy left to us by countless seekers is that we too can access the insights and direct experiences that lead to awakening. They are equally available to everyone who passionately and persistently pursues expansion and liberation. The question is: How do we translate this wisdom into our own daily lives? Do those of us who are born to perform in the corporate world need to leave the boardroom and go to India for three years? Fortunately, the answer is, "Not necessarily."

The inhibition and restriction that we have referred to as bondage are keenly felt whenever we need new definitions and perspectives to better respond to life's demand that we expand ourselves. But we now have the tools and understanding to deconstruct our concepts and assumptions and free ourselves right where we are in the corporate playground. Today's global culture has blessed us with the expanded sense that we can demand processes that benefit us personally as well as our companies. In fact, it's often hard to tell when what we call a personal activity has left off and a corporate one begins. In addition, the use of pointers to enter into our own experience has the handy feature of being portable. Add these two ingredients to the recipe of adult maturation and transformation, and you have the possibility of an awakening right here and right now. This has always been the case, but now we find ourselves in an emerging tide that supports that possibility in the corporate world. So what does it look like to forge this frontier?

We might begin to answer that question by looking at how I operate in this environment. My work over the past twelve or thirteen years has been to act as a doorway—commonly referred to as a coach—to the transformation, or awakening, process. It is apparent from my experience that this type of deep work can happen for any leader who is sufficiently motivated. My goal in this chapter is to illustrate to you how such a process can be accessed and how it can unfold.

In our discussions about the ego, it has become evident that the first step in any personal process is to find our blind spots—that is, our conditionings as they developed in childhood in response to our early environment. These are held in the unconscious, ready to spring forth whenever a triggering situation arises. Since these early-stage conditionings cause our responses to occur automatically, we refer to ourselves as being "in reaction" when we are triggered. The triggering, and our reactive response to it, happens on its own because the parts of our human machinery known as awareness and reflection remain submerged underneath the unconscious need to defend ourselves against feeling pain. The energy that could be directed toward more adaptive and creative behaviors remains stuck in our repetitive defensive patterns, and the behaviors that result from our reactive tendencies block the positive outcomes that we desire.

So the first objective on the path called transformation is to build the bridge out of reactive responses and into the realm of creative activity— that is, behaviors that can be lived when an ego is no longer in unconscious bondage to its early conditionings. In order for that to happen, we need to understand more clearly the nature of reactivity, starting with its primary characteristic: Reactive tendencies are almost always deeply hidden and, what's more, resistant to being discovered.

Why are reactive tendencies hidden? You might think that it is because we all want to avoid feeling ashamed or embarrassed. Or because we are afraid that any revelation of weakness or dysfunction will adversely affect others' opinions and assessments of our worth in the workplace—or our value simply as human beings. These may be real considerations, but what I want to point to here is the deeper, underlying reason: *The ego wants to be ahead of where it actually is in the maturation process.* Most people are intelligent enough to see that reactive behaviors are childish. But it is more alluring to pretend that one is further down the line in the maturation process than it is to go back and identify the source of these behaviors. So the ego buries its responses in the graveyard of unwanted behaviors without ever resolving its immaturity. The cemetery, however, is filled with live attributes that have merely been judged to be dead; as in a B-grade horror flick, they all come out to play in the dark.

In the corporate world, you won't find work groups dedicating days on end to exhuming these traits from the burial ground in which they lie. Few, if any, companies would be willing to commit to processes that would disengage, even temporarily, the drivetrain operating the entity called the company—how can they conduct business as usual if the employees are ensconced in process rooms day and night? Plus, in our Western culture, we tend to live in measured blocks of time, dedicating certain hours to specific tasks penciled into the little windows in our daily schedule. During a typical work week, personal hygiene gets an hour as the day begins, followed by your commute, four hours of morning work and meetings, an hour for lunch, and another work block in the afternoon, and then the trip home again. If you've got a family, the children get the back end of the day, perhaps competing with TV, surfing the Web, or other interests. If you're lucky, you can squeeze in some time for the gym or to meet with friends. It is into this type of structure that we now must place the process of awakening. What type of device can we find that functions within these blocks of time?

The most common and widely used tool, the 360-degree personal profile, is a personality assessment device that comes in myriad forms. Many of the ones currently in use collect data supplied by the candidate and a chosen set of feedback providers. A series of questions are designed to draw out information on how the candidate is perceived, both by himself and the other participants, and the results are compiled into a written report. Sometimes, handing the report to an individual is the sum total of the discovery process. In other cases, it is reviewed together by coach and client and corrective behaviors are suggested, based on characteristics that have been found to be problematic or less than ideal. But we have already seen that reactive tendencies hide in the unconscious. So even the delivery of a report that reveals reactive tendencies, accompanied by a punch list of suggested improvements, is rarely sufficient for any real, lasting change to occur. And it almost never opens the way for a true discovery process. Why? Because a good reporting tool needs to access the unconscious and engage the intuition.

In my coaching, I use the 360-degree personal profile assessment by The Leadership Circle, which is designed to highlight reactive tendencies and serve as an entryway into an intuitive discovery process. The candidate not only answers an in-depth series of queries relating to his behavior, he also selects ten to twelve working partners, bosses, direct reports, and other coworkers to answer the same series of questions about him.

Why, you may ask, do we solicit the input from others? Because while all of us are unconscious of some of our traits, the people around us can usually see them as though they were illuminated by the noonday sun. All the responses are compiled and represented in a circular diagram where reactive tendencies appear in the bottom half and the creative competencies are at the top, with percentile summary scores given for all dimensions of leadership. This depiction reflects the recognition that reactive tendencies, which are obstacles to maturity, lie beneath the conscious mind. It is this maturity that must be developed in order for a leader to reach his awakened potential.

The Leadership Circle Profile tool is designed to be much more than an interesting, or even an informative, graph filled with data. Bob Anderson, the thought leader of this company, created it specifically to allow coaching candidates to directly experience their own reactive tendencies, not just hear about them. It is meant to evoke from the person being coached the experiential responses that remain largely controlled or completely hidden during the course of their interactions with others in the workplace. Even though most people cannot see their reactive behaviors coming, we can count on the fact that, given the proper trigger, those behaviors will always arise in the debriefing portion of the process. These reactive responses point right to where the coaching process needs to start in order to make a real difference in the person's relationships and performance.

The example of a young female CEO of an outdoor-products company—let's call her Betty—illustrates the profound transformation that this method can produce. The outdoor-products business is largely populated by men—men who like tents, sleeping bags, and thick-soled climbing boots. Betty, who had to perform in this largely male atmosphere, was known as a remarkable talent within the industry, but she had the reputation of being a caged tiger in times of crisis. Her team members were afraid to get too close to her because they sensed that they could end up as prey when times got tough. Betty knew something was amiss when she realized that she wasn't being effective in the situations that mattered most. So she decided to ask for some coaching to address the issue.

Betty is a petite, feminine woman with dark hair and penetrating blue eyes. Her intelligence is obvious. She is comfortable directing those around her and does so like the captain of a ship, her physical stature notwithstanding. But she knew that she needed a point of view that she could not access herself, which made her the perfect candidate for coaching. Still, when I suggested that she take the 360-degree personal profile, she balked; she was sure that she had taken every assessment known to man—how would one more make a difference? However, she was sufficiently driven to find a solution to the problem, so she agreed to the test. I explained the mechanics of the process and scheduled an appointment for our debriefing.

By the time we met, she was more than ready. But when I showed her the large gap between her self-image and the assessments of her handpicked respondents, the recoil was obvious. The profile shouted loud and clear that her main reactive tendency was to control, and that she was projecting her drive to be perfect onto her team members. She had worked hard all her life to manage her controlling style, yet it was still there for all to see. This was so difficult for her to take in that she couldn't help but blurt out, "There must be some mistake; are you sure this profile is mine?"

It is this type of visceral response that immediately lets me know that I have uncovered an unconscious behavior. *Reactivity is the vociferous denial that accompanies the unveiling of unwanted, unconscious behaviors.* A leader can never track these elements of their own leadership, much less transform them, until they are revealed.

When Betty recovered from her knee-jerk reaction, she became interested in understanding how this reactive tendency had developed out of her childhood conditioning. It seems that she had four brothers and a highly successful father. She had learned that the only way to make everyone around her happy was to control her environment and become a relentless perfectionist. In times of crisis, she became the delivery mechanism for enforced perfection, and her immediate family had bought in to, and even compensated for, that behavior. Her accounting for all the particulars and assembling them in a perfect pattern had policed the male hierarchy surrounding her at home. This behavior, which was accentuated whenever the pressure was on, naturally spilled over at the office. If some control was good, more control must be better. As with all behavior, this pattern had surfaced automatically and became self-operating—but now it was manifesting in an environment that was not eager to accommodate her shrill, attacking manner. When a different approach was needed, it was nowhere to be found.

When Betty could recognize the same reactivity in her management style that she had with her family when she was young, she immediately understood the problems between herself and her team, because that childhood pattern had been reclaimed into her felt experience. It was no longer unconscious.

Whenever someone becomes aware of a reactive tendency, there will almost always be a moment of shock and awe such as Betty experienced. I can tell you that seldom will someone forget that moment; remember, for all of our lives we been unconsciously avoiding any encounter with these tendencies. But the outbreak of an experiential discovery is the most significant point in the entire sequence of events in the coaching relationship that leads to disidentification. Why? Because it indicates where the process of transformation can begin. So, while the tool itself is important for uncovering what has been hidden, it is in the coaching process itself that the self-discovery and bridging to the subsequent steps occur.

Betty's story illustrates how important it is that our intuition always illuminate the way forward in the transformative process. In contrast, our corporate culture has enshrined reports, data, and technology often to the detriment of our own natural intuitive insight. In creating his assessment tool, Bob Anderson recognized this problem and encouraged coaches to keep the central focus on intuition. He describes here the principles that form the basis of his system:

> In System Dynamics Theory, structure determines performance. In other words, the primary determinate of the performance of any system is the design of that system. Underneath the design of the system is the thinking and assumptions that formed the design. In other words, thinking creates the design, and design determines the performance. We call this thinking behind the design, deep structure. In human terms, deep structure is the system of the thinking that drives a leader's pattern of behavior. Deep structure is the Leader's Operating System.
>
> The Leadership Circle Profiles are designed to surface deep structure. They create a platform that allows us to inquire into the beliefs and assumptions that are the source-code for the pattern of behavior— as measured in the competency data. The benefits of this approach are obvious: accessing the underlying assumptions that drive behavior

creates the opportunity to redesign the operating system. This allows the desired leadership effectiveness to develop naturally.[1]

Bob's explanation is written in a language familiar to those of us who have been exposed to corporate theory. But it contains the same essence, the same understanding, that I have been describing throughout this book: The ego is a collection of characteristics that are brought into existence based on assumptions that are made about the environment in which it lives. These assumptions, like the ego itself, become unconscious and drive our behavior and form what Bob calls our operating system. But we have seen that this operating system can be shifted if we can dissolve our identification with it. This is the understanding that opens the door to our transformation. What better way to see how leadership theory and ancient awakening processes are not only intertwined, they are one and the same in their thrust to create a shift that will dissolve identification?

The 360-degree tool is not limited to pinpointing reactive behavior and unconscious assumptions; neither the profile itself nor the coaching process is aimed at fixing dysfunction. Within the stages of adult maturation is a pull or yearning toward the pole of awakening, also called the unitive. The opening created in the coaching experience is aimed at the movement into the creative domain and beyond. Yes, the first experience is typically a painful disclosure of unseen ego-identification. But within that disclosure can also be found the trigger that drives the movement into awakening.

Some time ago, I was asked to coach a senior operations executive for one of the largest apparel companies in the world. Harold had spent his whole career in the operations side of this industry, beginning at the age of fourteen. He had come up through the ranks and had done each of those functions himself along the way, so all of his direct reports had a powerful affinity for him. His goal was to continue his ascent up the ladder and into the executive ranks of his company, but he was encountering some difficulty along the way because he wasn't being clearly understood by those to whom he reported. As one might expect, his profile reflected this. But the gap between how his direct reports saw him and how his superiors characterized him was greater than I had ever seen in a profile.

A normal approach might be to thoroughly analyze the data and get to work changing those behaviors that Harold's superiors found problematic, ignoring this large difference. But when he was told that the test results indicated that his superiors saw him as controlling and autocratic, he intuited that something was amiss. Some coaches might push an employee to own any trait that shows up in the profile. But by holding space for Harold to make his own discovery, it became apparent that in questioning this finding, he was on to something.

We know that in ego development, blind spots will be installed in our childhood experience. And we have seen that because we typically don't have the tools to make them conscious, we simply pretend in our adult years that these attributes are no longer at play. This is called denial. This denial must then be interrupted via a discovery process of one kind or another. But Harold's objection to his superiors' assessment of him was not denial at all; rather, it was an intuitive sense that needed to be respected and then explored. Unlike Betty, when confronted with the assertion that he was controlling and autocratic, Harold did not display any of the reactions that I have come to expect when the imputation of a reactive behavior is right on target. This cued me to dig a little deeper with him.

Harold is an introverted personality with a penchant for compliance. He is really good at what he does. These traits had served him well in the inventory, manufacturing, and operations arenas. So we began to discuss the nature of his relationships with his direct reports compared with his behavior toward his superiors. As we explored further, we discovered that, as a result of seeing himself as a common working guy, Harold was prone to hide himself from his superiors. That is to say, he had not learned how to reflect his personality upward, whereas he warmly held, and was warmly held by, all those who reported to him.

If you have ever worked in mass production, you know that this is a common behavior; I experienced it myself as a teenager working in the Sunkist packinghouse. Harold had learned it in the textile-cutting plants where he had been seasoned. So it was obvious to me that it was entirely possible for him to be seen vastly differently by these two groups within the same company. But that didn't answer the next question: Why did his superiors see him as autocratic and controlling?

The answer was to be found in the personality profiles of Harold's bosses. It turns out that in this company, as in many organizations, the executive core was composed of leaders with high levels of controlling, autocratic, reactive characteristics. As dictated by a career trajectory that either directly or indirectly supported this, Harold had been hiding his best behavioral characteristics from his superiors, presenting a blank slate to them. When given an empty canvas, what will an ego paint? It will fill the space with the features it is most familiar with—that is to say, its own reactive tendencies. So the executive team to whom Harold reported could see no other characteristics in him besides the ones that they themselves would have mobilized had they been in his position.

This explanation may seem to be merely an intellectual rendering of the characteristics of Harold's superiors. But our discovery changed his entire approach to his career. Together, we were able to correctly iden-tify his reactive characteristics and design a program to expand those into the creative space, without stumbling over and wasting time trying to deal with problems that he did not have. And all that was needed to rectify the imbalance in how people perceived him across all levels of the company was for Harold to begin communicating upward his real per-sonality, especially the creative traits that he could deploy on behalf of the business. For a naturally introverted and compliant individual such as Harold, this needed to include a communication program, so we came up with several methods that would fill in the blanks for his superiors. Like the caravan leader in our story in chapter 15, Harold just needed to show his superiors the rock. But in this case, the rock was not an obstacle; rather, it was the evidence of his value to the company. He was already more of a leader than anybody was aware of—as well as a hidden resource. He just needed to let them know.

Every coaching session begins with the experience of a coach sitting across from a human being who believes that he or she is an individual ego juxtaposed with—and sometimes opposed to—all other objects and people within the world that he or she inhabits. A coach, however, should know that these apparent divisions do not exist within the creative space and beyond. So rather than acting as another participant or object in the drama, *the coach becomes the doorway to the creative space simply by being at one with the field of unity that is present in every meeting between individuals.* In the language common to spiritual seekers, I would say that for this to happen, an environment of satsang, the same one that I enjoyed at the feet of the masters, must be created. For it is through holding space that a coach helps the seeker to find her own hidden reactive tendencies.

A critical step toward this type of breakthrough is the transition in acceptance. It is in accepting the truth of what is that we expand, allowing reactive traits to shift and move into the creative arena. And this natural expansion will flow into an awareness of other reactive characteristics, which can then be transformed as well. For expansion, in its very essence, is a beckoning and an invitation to follow the course of our natural unfoldment. It could be said that everything that happens or arises in any coaching process that is modeled on the experience of being in satsang does so in a space that is held by Source. Even if today's corporate thought leaders have never heard these terms before, the outcome—not just for the coaching process but in any area of leadership—is fast becoming a recognizable destination.

In order to get there, you don't need to stand naked on a stage in an Indian ashram and recite a list of your shadow traits, as I did; everything you need to see can be revealed in your own office or boardroom as part of the coaching relationship. With the simple recognition that each reactive characteristic does indeed house itself in your ego, an acceptance becomes seeded in you that will eventually blossom into the very field of wholeness. Within that field, your various attributes—whether you see them as positive or negative—will continue to arise, but never again with the intensity of identification that marks them as unconscious and reactive.

The examples of Harold and Betty reveal essentially the same ego dynamics that are faced by seekers on the personal path of awakening; the externals look different, but the issues are no different on the corporate path of leadership. There is no dividing line; those of us who were built by nature for the corporate playing field also stand squarely on the path of personal seeking. And no matter what those who don't identify with corporate achievement as a place to flower may claim, or how they may seek to draw lines that do not exist, we know by our own irresistible attraction to the world of achievement that we are in our right place. As the false lines of demarcation disappear, the natural seekers in the corporate terrain are standing up to ask for the experiences that they intuitively know will bring them to acceptance, and then beyond, to the point of awakening. These experiences must, and will, contain the elements that both spiritual giants and corporate thought leaders have long extolled.

18 Doorways to Awakening

We began our journey many chapters ago with the story of how the ego of a child named Alan came into being and developed over the course of a typical personal history. Then, in our discussions about presence, service, and relationships, we came to see that what we really are is not the ego-created and -defined self but the container, the spaceholder, from which all of our life experience can emerge. Finally, in chapter 17, we sampled some ways in which the personal work that leads to awakening can unfold through devices available to us in the corporate world. However, even after this long journey, you might not yet have developed a sense for the distance between yourself as the witness versus being the author of your own actions. A false sense of doership may still be filling the entire space of your felt experience. If that is the case, Awakened Leadership will, of course, still seem to be out of reach. That is because *nothing that you will ever want is within the grasp of your ego*.

This was the insight that allowed me to begin to create space in my own awareness for the ego to be seen for what it is. Up until my time at the commune in India, my only approach to new experiences was to formulate a goal, come up with a strategy, create a list of things to do, and then execute them point by point. If you recall, when I sat myself across from the Multiversity counselor on my first day at the commune, he asked if I needed time to arrive. In ashram-speak, he was implying that I probably hadn't settled in and wasn't ready to begin a journey into direct experience. I did not yet have a sense of myself that could understand what he was getting at, so in my usual fashion, I immediately came out with the equivalent of, "Sure, I've arrived. I'm sitting here, aren't I?" After reading twelve chapters of my life story and another four in which the examples and metaphors are more conceptually grounded, you are probably in a much better position than I was to enter into the passage from identification to awakening. This chapter is your invitation into that passage—via a process that is uniquely your own.

This passage contains traffic signals that we to refer as pointers. I call them pointers because they are not rules or rigid directives, nor are they prods to complete assignments targeted toward a prescribed outcome. And they have not been organized into a system of numbered, graded steps for the ego to pounce on and execute as it has in the past. They are accessways from concept to experience. These pointers will, however, give your mind enough of a conceptual framework to satisfy its addiction to definitions and directives and to calm its need for intellectual understanding. Any of these pointers can open the door to this calming and relaxation of the mind. Inside that relaxation is the possibility that something radically new can happen that will take you beyond any conceptual framework.

Because each one of you is different, your experiences will vary. But in the end, the breakthrough is the same for everybody. It can be best described as a felt experience of the absence of the boundaries that we have created through the definitions and beliefs that we once held as true and immutable. This means that your experiences along the way will contain elements of the unknown. Bear in mind that this unknown is as much a part of your composition as your known ego. It is through these early contacts with the unknown that your experience of the ego, which is so binding, can be seen, accepted, and integrated as a part of a larger experience.

This chapter is designed to help you understand the function of pointers and how they relate to Awakened Leadership. So don't go looking for merit badges or red hatchets. Simply let each pointer settle in. Two sensitivities are needed here: allowing and watching. As I describe a pointer, just notice what comes up for you. You will be surprised by the new awareness this will bring to your normal style of inquiry. And when it is time to engage in a particular practice, I invite you to approach it with an attitude of letting discovery find you.

Although the suggestions in this chapter are meant to lead you into direct experiences, you are not going to arrive at any particular location. However, these pointers do invite you to *start* someplace—and that place is wherever you are in the moment. Whatever questions you have as you approach the door to your our own personal passageway are the perfect questions for opening it. As you begin your walk, remember that your first pointer might be located at any position on the corridor of awakening; if another pointer seems like a better place to start than the first one discussed below, by all means, go for it. Every pointer is an equal-access opportunity—and its own invitation—to Awakened Leadership.

This may be your first exploration outside of the realm of doership. Welcome to the mystery of your own journey.

☞ *Your viewpoint is only a stop along the way*

We have already confirmed that all concepts are open to interpretation and, therefore, can never contain all of what is. But how does this understanding become a pointer toward your own availability to a breakthrough? As your ego developed, everyone and everything around you underscored again and again that concepts are either true or false. Through that conditioning, you have taken on the unconscious behavior of staunchly advocating your own position in relation to any concept that catches your interest. Most conversations, and certainly all media interactions, are based on this type of interchange. The moment a topic surfaces, people immediately take sides, marshaling the so-called facts to passionately support their viewpoint. They even believe that raising their voice adds to the power of their position.

It is important to understand here that viewpoints do not exist as independent phenomena; they always arise out of an ego to which they are connected. The ego is the platform that the view is being seen from.

Once you are aware of this, an easy device can be used to make this habit of defending your views more conscious. The next time you find yourself in such a conversation, notice how it feels to be fighting for your side of the argument. We are used to insisting on our point of view because we believe that there is such a thing as absolute truth. This behavior, which is energetically matched by the other side, continues to confirm for you that beliefs and positions are either right or wrong, true or false.

As soon as you find yourself gearing up to take on all comers, see whether you can become aware of the sense that accompanies the belief that you are right. You may only have been vaguely aware of this, but whenever you are in the midst of this type of discussion, a felt experience with specific characteristics is always present. Begin by noticing when you have started fighting to defend a concept, and gently stay in that place. Without forcing yourself to change anything, observe any changes in your physical body. What is happening to your breathing? Have your eyes narrowed their focus? How have the tempo and pitch of your voice changed? What do you notice about your musculature? Is your physical stance different from how it usually is?

Once you have taken note of all these things, your awareness will be sufficiently expanded for you to make a shift and take a different approach. Simply begin to consider that the argument does not need to have a specific outcome. From there you can move into the space of hearing an assertion of truth as one of several possibilities. With practice, you will gradually expand beyond knee-jerk responses when your own beliefs are challenged, and your capacity to see and appreciate multiple viewpoints in the course of any argument or disagreement will grow exponentially. In fact, by adding or subtracting variables, you can immediately change the parameters of the disagreement itself. At a certain point, you will find yourself capable of simply letting the conversation be whatever it is. And you will be able to register the difference between the experience of fighting as an ego versus looking with a wider-lens curiosity at how various people perceive a given situation.

In addition to noticing your tendency to fight for concepts as though they were absolute truths, also observe when you are doing this without forethought. This is called being in reaction. Becoming conscious of your reactivity may not be easy at first because your defensive and offensive responses are often set off before you realize how desperate you are to hold your ground, win the argument, or best the other guy. As you become more capable of identifying reactive behavior, you get better at placing some distance between yourself and your reactions. You become the subject of your own observation—your own social-science experiment, if you will. As you begin to increase your capacity to watch yourself, your availability to engage in a conversation with reactive human beings and remain nonreactive yourself will increase.

☞ *Contrary to all appearances, you are not the doer*

Awakening is the shift from doership to holding space. When this occurs, leadership emanates from an entirely different platform. There is no sense of personal doing but rather a sense of allowing. That shift creates a sense of presence that can be felt by those you lead. Then all of your behaviors become creative responses to what is, not an attempt to control yourself, other people, and your world.

As we have seen, the spyglass effect is what occurs when you see yourself and your own concerns to the exclusion of the wider field that is present at any given moment. Here, too, our conditioning is so deep and has been in effect for so long, that this felt sense of ourselves is difficult to escape. We have become convinced that we are the authors of our own decisions, plans, and activities. That is to say, we think that we are not only *a* doer, we are *the prime and exclusive* doer. So we need an approach that will deemphasize the single, all-important object called "me."

Here is a practice that can take you a long way toward the direct recognition that the ego is just one among many objects that are present and perceivable in the constantly changing field of your experience. Pick a time during the day when you know that you will be with other people for a specific block of time—a meeting at work or perhaps lunch with colleagues or friends. Remind yourself beforehand to widen your perception throughout that interaction so that you can sense not only yourself but also everything and everyone else that appears with you at that time. This might initially seem difficult to do, but after some practice, you will start to notice the difference between periods when your attention is focused predominantly or exclusively on yourself and those times when you have a more inclusive vision.

Notice the difference between these two states. How do you respond to the people and objects in each one? Practice this with groups and settings of various sizes and observe what tends to loop you back into self-focused participation. Gradually, you will be able to experience more of the world from a wide-perception perspective.

Here is another exercise that can help you to move the lens that is stuck on yourself to the exclusion of everything else; it was Ramesh's favorite. Choose a time after the day's events have come to their natural completion and dedicate half an hour to do the following. Select from everything that has happened that day the most positive event or outcome for which you believe you are responsible. Then begin to examine this event, noting all of the factors that had to be in place in order for it to occur. The more of these you can identify, the better. Then for each of these, begin to list all the things you can think of that were necessary for *them* to occur. At each level, you will most likely need to list dozens of variables over which you had no control. This part of the exercise can take you into an almost infinite regression.

After your half hour is over, ask yourself this question: "Am I still completely convinced that I created the outcome of the event that I selected?" You will be surprised to see how much your felt experience of the event has changed from what it was at the beginning of the exercise.

A variation of this practice is to focus on the outcome that you are most unhappy about or dissatisfied with. Go through the above steps and ask yourself the same questions. Notice that when the event you picked was positive, the ego wanted to lay claim to the outcome, whereas when the event was perceived as negative, you most likely wanted to disavow any ownership of it. But in both cases, you saw yourself as the prime mover in the situation.

When I played on the offensive line of my high school football team, one of my best friends was selected to be quarterback. Bill was one of the most gifted athletes in our school and also had a vibrant, outgoing personality. An intelligent quarterback understands that a good offensive line is one of the major contributors to his success. This is because the job of that group is to ensure that no one breaks through to tackle the quarterback before he can direct the offense of the team. But it had not occurred to Bill that his line was the reason why he had time to do his job; he thought that his talent alone was the cause of the team's success.

Toward the end of my first season on the team, my fellow linemen began to grumble about this. So they hatched a little plot to help Bill take notice of their existence. During a game that the whole team knew we could easily win, a couple of our linemen deliberately let an opposing all-star defensive lineman through during the first quarter, which resulted in Bill being tackled immediately. This was repeated a few more times. By halftime, Bill realized that this was not happening by accident. When we gathered in the locker room, he could tell from the silly grins on our faces that we, the linemen, were responsible. The jig was up. Bill's sense of humor allowed him to laugh as loudly as we did. This experience bonded Bill and our offensive team for the rest of the season. I would guess that if he had gone home that evening and reviewed the events for which he felt solely responsible, he probably would have arrived at an entirely new point of view about himself as both a quarterback and a member of the team. It would have been impossible, given this experience, to claim sole credit for any triumph.

So, when you do the exercise for this pointer, consider yourself and the people on your team—it could be a work group, your family, a social group, a public service committee, or any other group you are a part of—and see how your perception of yourself shifts. You don't need to get tackled by the largest defensive lineman on your own playing field in order to get the point.

☞ *You are enough—let your power come to you*

Regardless of how difficult or complex a given process or challenge may be, developing leaders and seekers always bring an earnestness and single-minded focus to the table that naturally releases their inherent power. In my younger days, I was part of a national love affair with what we called muscle cars. My favorite was the 1967 Pontiac GTO. It had a sleekness and beauty on the outside that was pleasing enough, but when you lifted the hood, there sat a gleaming power plant that was a miracle to behold. Anyone with an appreciation for engineering and machinery could see at a glance that these cars meant business. Their job was to achieve the fastest possible speed in the shortest amount of time. When the engine roared to a start, you could feel in your own body the sheer muscular potential that was about to be unleashed.

I have often thought that leaders who follow their intuitive sense of internal expansion are built like muscle cars. They have one purpose that never leaves their awareness and they always seem ready to launch into the race at the drop of a flag. I am not the first coach or advisor to point toward this quality. But I want you to see it in an entirely different way. When someone suggests that you look for your purpose or passion, in most cases the ego takes the suggestion as its next assignment. In fact, long days and nights are consumed as doers construct their versions of passion and attempt to drop those into their life as newfound discoveries that merely generate more fuel for the ego. I am trying to convey to you a much deeper sense. The simple fact that you are reading material about leadership and awakening tells me that you probably have a muscle car engine lurking under your hood. My suggestion is to not accelerate toward a goal or an outcome that you define, but rather to allow the earnestness that is already in you to fully surface.

The next exercise is an invitation to focus your awareness exclusively on yourself. In this self-examination, first take a look inside and see whether that power engine is there. Once you have established that you are in the muscle car category, note how it feels to be in contact with your own power. What does it actually feel like in your body? It is this felt experience that can become the platform of your internal expansion. Once you can sense even a small difference between yourself and the power that drives you, that observation becomes the doorway to expansion. You will become conscious of the difference between power that is an extension of your essential self and the power that you, as an ego, attempt to control.

Now notice whether you are automatically inclined to harness that horsepower to a particular objective. Is it possible for you to simply remain with the felt sense of your own power without having to do anything with it? If so, what happens to it? Does it intensify? Diminish? Remain steady? Try allowing it to be there simply as the capacity to see yourself more clearly rather than using it to assess or solve a specific problem you may be facing. Notice how your sense of your own awareness and presence shifts when you do this.

Some years ago, a Russian teenager was scheduled to play in the finals of a tennis tournament against one of the greatest players of all time. The youngster was so far down in the rankings that he was hardly noticed. In the final match, the inconceivable occurred—he beat his opponent. After his victory, he was barraged by reporters pressing him to reveal the strategy behind this amazing feat. To everyone's surprise, he responded—I'm paraphrasing here—I didn't use any strategy at all. My opponent was such a champion, I knew that coming up with a particular game plan would be useless. So, I decided that when I stepped out on the court, I would do only one thing: Every time a ball came across the net, I would simply hit it back.

His single-focused purpose was not a coaching prescription that he was trying to fulfill but a realization of a particular quality demanded by the game itself. Through his participating as just another part of the game rather than as an identified competitor, the outcome created itself. This capacity for holding space for the natural unfolding of events exists within every leader and seeker that I have coached or encountered. Rather than create a conceptually structured passion that needs to be translated into a specific strategy, find what already is there and allow its full expression. This is how you become available to your own breakthrough.

☞ *A leader needs no followers*

All of the pointers that we are discussing are aimed at moving your felt experience of a single ego/doer to the unified field of doing that arises in every moment. A question that might come to mind is, "How can I be a leader if all I am is one object within a group of assorted objects? Doesn't that disregard the uniqueness of my contribution?" Not in the least. All objects—including your ego—that arise at any given time, in any situation, retain their natural character and will operate based on their own attributes. By allowing this to be the case, you will naturally expand into the position that we call holding space rather than jockeying for position and influence. The beauty of this expansion is that you get to experience all of the supposed doers in your world being lived into the function that they were designed to fulfill. This expanded felt experience eliminates the sense of a variety of players independently exerting their best efforts as single doers.

Once you have made this shift, you can easily see that to be an awakened leader is to allow leadership to arise in you as who you really are in any moment when leadership is called out. Without any worry, you can rely on the fact that the leadership qualities you have already developed within your body-mind cannot help but to come into play. An awakened leader is simply the character that plays her part as a function of the entire happening.

From this perspective, it can be seen that the human ability to colonize multiple objects within the container called leadership is interesting but irrelevant. The characteristics of Awakened Leadership come into play and will be naturally expressed whether the field consists of only yourself or thousands of other actors that you are leading. It couldn't happen any other way.

☞ *Let life live you*

Recently, my coaching partner, Bob Bunshaft, sent me one of his blog posts to review. I was immediately struck by the title: "I am not the Doer, but I am open to suggestions." I must confess that I don't remember much from the text of his blog—the title said it all. In one sentence, Bob had pointed to the doorway that takes one from doership to leadership.

It is easy to see the difference between grabbing a bull by the horns and letting that same bull nibble feed from your hand. That difference is the essence of all pointers. It is also the doorway beyond self-mastery and into Awakened Leadership. We have been told that we must turn the world upside down to find our passion and then treat it as a call to action that our ego must complete. But in the new land of leadership, where old boundaries no longer qualify, we can see that the natural desire of any leader is already there and ready to go. There is no need to search for it. If we will simply notice that we, as leaders, naturally lead within the emergence of any set of events, we will also take note that our desires, along with those of all the other players, can naturally propel everyone in the field toward a result that does not get derailed by self-interest. All of our leadership attributes will arise along with our desires, and we will be the space within which everything that is needed comes to everybody who is present.

This is the difference between leadership as a doing and leadership emerging naturally. When you cross this threshold, you will taste the experience of Awakened Leadership. And you will see that it doesn't matter whether the crowd is following you or you are the only one in the caravan—leadership is your natural birthright.

That is when the ultimate and timeless question arises: Are you ready to let life live you?

Afterword

One of my favorite authors is Joseph Jaworski, author of *Synchronicity: The Inner Path of Leadership*.[1] Mr. Jaworski has now written a follow-on volume titled *Source: The Inner Path of Knowledge Creation*. I read the following description of this new work in a book catalog.

> Institutions of all sorts are facing profound change today, with complexity increasing at a speed and intensity we've never experienced before. Jaworski came to realize that traditional analytical leadership approaches are inadequate for dealing creatively with this complexity. To effectively face these challenges, leaders need to access the Source from which truly profound innovation flows.
>
> Many people, including Jaworski himself, have experienced a connection with this Source, often when called upon to respond in times of crisis—moments of extreme spontaneity and intuitive insight. Actions simply flow through them, seemingly without any sort of conscious intervention. They don't think about what they do; they just *know*. But these experiences are chance occurrences—ordinarily, we don't know how to access the Source, and we even have a blind spot as to its very existence.[2]

It is clear that the most advanced writings on leadership are now inviting us to tap in to the Source of all vision and inspiration. I gladly join the choir of voices that see this possibility. But additional steps can be taken beyond even the capacity to access Source. We have discovered in our time together that the ego and Source melt into the same field.

That is because they were never really separate—we were only holding it that way. First, we discover that all that happens or arises does so in a space that is actually Source. And then, usually when we least expect it, we discover that we have stepped into Source itself—which is the experience of our awakening. Knowing that this awakening occurs in the natural progression of the combined spiritual and corporate journeys opens us to the ultimate possibility of our own future as awakened beings and awakened leaders.

So let's begin to acknowledge that our life, as we know it, is handing us a gift of possibility. It's time to celebrate the newly arising recognition that we are no longer required to pursue our heartfelt internal goals anywhere else than where we love to be.

My message to you is that your journey is authentic no matter where it takes place. If you're a corporate animal, much like myself, then that is the arena in which your search unwinds. Everything you need to reach home is already within the world you inhabit, for Source is everywhere. And consciousness is all there is.

Notes

Chapter 3

1. "Primary Headache Goes on Mission," *Corona Ward News for June 1972* (newsletter for the Third Quorum of Elders Presidency), Corona Ward, Corona, CA.

Chapter 8

1. Osho, *Tantra: The Supreme Understanding* (London: Watkins Publishing, 2009), text copyright Osho Foundation International, February 11, 1975 discourse.

Chapter 13

1. Maurice Frydman, trans.; rev. and ed. by Sudhakar S. Dikshit, *I Am That: Talks with Sri Nisargadatta Maharaj* (Durham, NC: The Acorn Press, 1973), 50.

Chapter 14

1. Maurice Frydman, trans.; rev. and ed. by Sudhakar S. Dikshit, *I Am That: Talks with Sri Nisargadatta Maharaj* (Durham, NC: The Acorn Press, 1973).

Chapter 17

1. Bob Anderson, "Searching in All the Wrong Places," *Leadership Quarterly*, April 2011, under section heading "Why Deep Structure?" on The Leadership Circle website, www.theleadershipcircle.com/content2249 (accessed August 11, 2011).

Afterword

1. Joseph Jaworski, *Synchronicity: The Inner Path of Leadership* (San Francisco: Berrett-Koehler Publishers, 1996).

2. Berrett-Koehler Fall 2011 Catalog, publisher's description of *Source: The Inner Path of Knowledge Creation* by Joseph Jaworski (San Francisco: Berrett-Koehler Publishers), 12.

Acknowledgements

I never set out to become a writer or author. But the doorway to the path of awakening opens onto many unexpected treasures. The pointers found in this book sprouted their way through the garden of my heart and onto paper as though they were writing themselves. I happily bow to the consciousness that I am and whose writing you will find herein.

Everyone who is mentioned here has shared in surrendering to the organic process of this book and the experiences that made it worth writing.

To my grandfather I will eternally be grateful. And the family he inspired was a beautiful nest: My grandmother, my mother, my father, and my brothers and sisters were all there in the beginning. I am thankful as well for those old souls who implanted the wisdom of the earth and fired a young man's imagination in the little village of Corona. My gratitude also goes to my beloved Peruvians, who helped me find the yearning of my heart that was just too big to contain. Later, my career blossomed and showered me with friends such as Glenn, Jerry, David, and Bob. It would dilute the feeling I have for these men to only call them colleagues.

My sense of family has expressed itself over time as an ever-expanding love. The intimacy I feel with Osho and Ramesh goes beyond merely honoring them as the venerable grandfathers of my spiritual family. And I have been lucky as a father and partner to have been in service to Justine, Lisa, Michael, and Kristin. I have also been sent beautiful souls in canine bodies, each seemingly calculated to teach me how to love. So when you see one of my little ones that need help, enthrone them in your heart, giving them names that will remain forever etched there, as these are in mine: Hercules, Xena, Odie, Bodhi, Lola, and Beso.

The work you hold in your hands appeared through the loving care of many beloveds. From the writer's cave where my editor, Elianne Obadia, and I ferreted out the shadows on the wall, the living message of this book arose. The writing happened as we were one within divine consciousness. This essence has now become the inspirational guide embracing a team of actors, each of whom surrendered to something greater than themselves. My gratitude goes to this special family of mine: Jayme Johnson of Worthy Marketing Group, Joel Friedlander of Marin Bookworks, Jeniffer Thompson of Monkey C Media, Rob Nissen of Nissen PR, and Jacqueline Simonds of Beagle Bay Inc. And a book could never be completed without those closest of friends who review and critique—and just won't take you seriously. Big thanks are due to Justine, who doubled as my copyeditor; Evelyn Treais, a publishing angel who appeared at the last minute; Benita Peters, who does anything that is needed; Bob Bunshaft, who still can't believe I wrote the book; Bob Anderson, who wrote the foreword; and Darrell Talbert, my brother from Corona, who wrote the preface and reviewed the book as though it were a thesis.

The people in my life who have dedicated themselves to our mission of Awakened Leadership are too many to mention, but they have each freely contributed to the message in this book. To all those who form my family in its infinite arisings, thank you. I love you all.

About the Author

Alan Shelton has lived a seemingly dual life of developing into a quintessential corporate manager while simultaneously engaging in the seeker's quest. Born in California, Alan grew up within the sixties' vision of infinite possibility. In his twenties, he worked tirelessly to master the nuts and bolts of his craft; within five years, he was at the pinnacle of his field.

Beginning at the age of thirty-eight, he spent four years over a ten-year period sitting with sages in India, blending his personal search with his love for the corporate adventure. These two territories had appeared to be incompatible, but in the wake of an event that permanently altered his perception and experience of reality, he realized that these worlds can be united in Awakened Leadership.

Observing that the leadership community is in the process of expanding its stewardship by demanding and creating a platform for personal development, he decided to write *Awakened Leadership*, using his life story as a laboratory. He sensed that the story of the development and subsequent relaxation of his ego could become both a pointer and an inspiration for others' awakening.

Central to Alan's world are the challenge and examination of the assumptions upon which people base their lives. Many presuppositions that are collectively held by our culture (corporate or otherwise) are responsible for both the lack of leadership and the discontent evident in society today. Alan has experienced the unwinding of these in his own awakening. Now his work centers on supporting others to deconstruct assumptions, thus opening the doorway to the possibility of living as the awakened self.

Alan is a living example among those who know that there is no difference between leadership and personal maturity. In fact, he is a product of transcending that long-held separation. It is from this perspective that Alan advises large multinational companies as well as the type of early-stage organizations that launched his highly successful merger/acquisition career. Alan began this career in 1977 at Price Waterhouse, where he was responsible for negotiating and structuring merger and acquisition transactions. Among his clients were IBM, Sunkist, Beckman Instruments, and Toyota Motor Sales. In 1984, as the senior partner of Shelton, Smith & Townsend, CPAs, Alan joined a CEO resource group called The Executive Committee (TEC), now known as Vistage, and remained a member until he sold his firm in 1990. This group included CEOs from Pacific Mutual, Allergan, Landsdale Carr, Vision Streetwear, and Quicksilver.

After a lifetime of managing organizations, Alan migrated to the leadership coaching area, where his talents could ignite those who are attempting to live authentically in the global corporate world. His current leadership assignments include VF Corporation, University of San Diego, and Celgene. In addition to his coaching practice, he holds gatherings for thirsty seekers who have the courage and passion to take a dip in the pool of intense experience.

Alan lives in a refurbished fire station in Oceanside, California, with his wife of seventeen years, Justine. She is a yoga therapist and healer who works with cancer survivors and individuals with chronic illness. His children—Kristin, twenty-eight, and Michael, twenty-six—graduated with business degrees from the University of Southern California and the University of Arizona, respectively, and are both avid entrepreneurs. Alan has had a long love affair with rescued dogs; as you are reading this, it is likely that he is in his office counseling clients, with the family dogs playing at his feet.